TOM PALMER

ULTIMATE
FOOTBALL HEROES

FOOTBALL'S
GREATEST MOMENTS

FROM THE PLAYGROUND
TO THE PITCH

T0273378

DINO

First published by Dino Books in 2023,
an imprint of Bonnier Books UK,
4th Floor, Victoria House, Bloomsbury Square, London WC1B 4DA
Owned by Bonnier Books,
Sveavägen 56, Stockholm, Sweden

🐦 @UFHbooks
🐦 @footieheroesbks
www.heroesfootball.com
www.bonnierbooks.co.uk

Paperback ISBN: 978 1 78946 715 4
E-book ISBN: 978 1 78946 719 2

British Library cataloguing-in-publication data:
A catalogue record for this book is available from the British Library.

Printed and bound in Great Britain by Clays Ltd, Elcograf S.p.A.

5 7 9 10 8 6

To Henry Robinson

ULTIMATE
FOOTBALL HEROES

Tom Palmer is the author of 58 books for children, including six
prize-winning WWI and WWII novels and four football series,
Roy of the Rovers, *Football Academy*, *Foul Play* and the *Soccer
Diaries*. He works in schools up and down the UK promoting
reading for pleasure through football. www.tompalmer.co.uk

Cover illustration by Dan Leydon.
To learn more about Dan, visit danleydon.com
To purchase his artwork visit etsy.com/shop/footynews
Or just follow him on Twitter @danleydon

ACKNOWLEDGEMENTS

Huge thanks to Henry Robinson (Mansfield Town &
Manchester City) and Simon Robinson (Nottingham
Forest), his dad, for being among the great football
minds I needed while writing this book. Thanks, too,
to David Allpress (Skircoat Green Physiotherapy) and
Dan Boots (Bradford City) for their contributions.
To Emil Fortune (Spurs) for making the planning,
writing and editing such a satisfying and fun process.
And to my agent, David Luxton (Leeds United) for
helping me write books about football and getting
paid for the pleasure.

AUTHOR'S NOTE

When you write a book about football's greatest moments, you're setting yourself up for people disagreeing with you. But that's fine. I think this. You think that. That's football.

We might agree on some of what I've included. Maradona. Marta. Messi. But we're going to disagree on plenty.

For instance, I will have left something out that does your head in. *How could he not include that? He knows nothing about football.* (Maybe I don't.) Or, *He dislikes my team and has left things out because of that.* (Maybe I do and have.)

Also, I might have included some things that really annoy you. Identify which team has way too many mentions in this book and you've probably worked out who I support.

What can I say? I'm sorry? I'm not sorry? You decide.

But, I hope you agree that this book contains most

of football's greatest moments from your point of view. Just not all. No apologies for that.

Thank you.
Tom (#MOT)

PERFECT ENDING

The argument about who is the greatest footballer that ever lived intensified as Lionel Messi's brilliant career evolved. Here was a man who had won the Ballon D'Or, the award for the year's greatest male footballer, seven times. But Messi had never lifted the World Cup. Could he be compared to Pelé and Maradona, football geniuses who had lifted the ultimate prize?

Messi was 35 when his last chance came: Qatar 2022. After unthinkably losing their opening game to Saudi Arabia, Messi's Argentina went on to beat Mexico, Poland, Australia, the Netherlands and Croatia. Now they faced the reigning champions, France, in the World Cup final. The two teams were so evenly matched that 90 minutes and extra time could not separate them. The winners of the 2022 men's World Cup – and Messi's legacy – would be decided on penalties.

Argentina needed to score with their last kick.

Messi waited with his teammates, a row of blue and white stripes, to see if he and they would achieve the ultimate stamp of greatness... or not.

GOALLLLLLLLLLLLLLLLLLL!!!!!!

The world changed in a moment. The penalty went in. The crowd roared. Most of the Argentina players rushed forward. But Lionel Messi dropped to his knees. On seeing him, his teammates doubled back, their arms encircling their captain, as every Argentina fan's arms encircled him in spirit. Maybe every football fan's.

Because those fans had just witnessed one of the greatest moments in football.

LIONEL MESSI	
Born	1987, Argentina
Position	Forward
Club goals	726
International goals	119
Selected honours	La Liga (10 times); Champion's League (4 times); World Cup

THE PERFECT BEGINNING

Pelé was at the beginning of his career when he played in his first World Cup final, against Sweden in 1958. The youngest player to play in the greatest game, he scored twice.

Pelé was just 17.

His first goal was one of the most outrageous goals ever scored in a World Cup final. The ball looped over to him from the left as he broke into the penalty area. He chested it down, beating the first defender. But a second defender closed him down, meaning he didn't have the space to shoot. So he chipped the ball over the Swede and, without allowing the ball to touch the ground, volleyed it into the back of the net.

His second goal came in the ninetieth minute, a deft header securing a 5–2 win and Brazil's first World Cup. Pelé had scored six goals during the tournament: one in the quarter-final, three in the semi, and now two in the final.

When the final whistle blew, he passed out, came round, then wept for joy. Pelé had become, and would remain, Brazil's greatest male footballer. In all, he would play in four World Cup tournaments, helping his country to win it three times: 1958, 1962 and 1970.

PELÉ	
Born	1940, Brazil
Position	Forward
Club goals	709
International goals	77
Selected honours	World Cup (3 times); FIFA Player of the Century

MARTA'S FIFTH

When the Brazilian footballer, Marta, won the FIFA World Player of the Year in 2010, she became the only footballer to win the ultimate individual award five years on the trot, dominating the award from 2006 to 2010 – something Messi, Pele and Maradona did not achieve. Then she won it again in 2018.

She was clearly the greatest ever female footballer. Playing professional football in Sweden, the USA and Brazil, Marta had an impossible combination of speed, power, touch and intelligence. She had everything.

Marta was the first to score in five World Cup final tournaments, an achievement matched only recently by Ronaldo in the men's World Cup. Her records and awards could fill a book on their own.

Although she was part of the Olympic Games winning team twice in 2004 and 2008, she never lifted the World Cup.

Nevertheless, Marta's fifth consecutive FIFA award

is undoubtedly still one of the greatest moments in football. And it came at a time that women's football and footballers were emerging from a time of unfair treatment.

MARTA	
Born	1986, Brazil
Position	Forward
Club goals	178
International goals	115
Selected honours	FIFA World Player of the Year (6 times)

POWER

When Scotland played England in 1881 at Easter
Road, Edinburgh, 1,000 fans showed up to watch.
But the newspaper coverage was full of contempt and
focused on the players' clothes and bodies, not the
football action.

It was a game between women.

The newspapers barely mentioned the great
historical moment of the first women's game under
the rules of association football, nor that Scotland
beat England 3–0 in the first women's international
football match. It was a time long before social media
and the internet. The men who wrote and published
newspapers had could tell the story just how
they wanted.

The teams played again in Glasgow a week later
and – wound up by the newspapers – men invaded
the pitch and rioted, throwing objects at the players,
forcing the game to be stopped.

A third game was cancelled.

There are records of more games between Scottish and English teams over this period, but little was written about it in the newspapers and little evidence remains. History is in the hands of those who have the power. Until those who have the power changes.

INTERNATIONAL FRIENDLY	
Saturday, 7 May 1881	
Scotland Ladies 3–0 England Ladies	
Lily St Clair	
Louise Cole	
Maud Randford	

TAKING THE KNEE

In 2016 the US footballer Megan Rapinoe put her career as an international footballer at risk. She 'took the knee' – in other words, she knelt during the playing of the American national anthem, rather than standing to attention, as was the tradition.

She did this to protest against the treatment of Black people by the police in the USA and to protest against racism generally.

Rapinoe used her fame and profile through football to make this protest. Rapinoe was the highest profile footballer in the USA and the most famous female footballer in the world. She could have been dropped by her club and country just for taking the knee.

Rapinoe had spoken about taking the knee. She says that white athletes don't feel the effects of the racism and that – even if it is not their fault – they, like everyone, all have the responsibility to challenge what is wrong.

HISTORICAL WRONG

The first Black player to be selected to play for the England men's team was a high-scoring Plymouth forward called Jack Leslie.

But he was dropped from the England team before the game took place.

Later in his life he remarked – in an interview and as an explanation – that 'they must have forgot I was a coloured boy'.

It was 1925. Leslie had been scoring a goal every three games for Plymouth and had come to the team selectors' attention. But – as he said – it is very likely that as soon as the Football Association became aware he was Black, he was removed from the team.

In 2022 a statue was put up at Plymouth's stadium, Home Park. In the same year the Football Association awarded Jack Leslie, who had died in 1988, the international cap he never received. Ninety-seven years later.

'The FA,' they said, 'is awarding Jack a posthumous honorary cap to recognise his unique contribution and set of circumstances – and to right the historical wrong.'

Sadly, Jack Leslie had died in 1988, some 34 years before the statue was erected and his posthumous cap was awarded.

JACK LESLIE	
Born	1901, England
Position	Forward
Club goals	133
Selected honours	Football League Third Division South

FIRST

The first Black player to play for the England first team was the Nottingham Forest full back, Viv Anderson.

Born in Nottingham he was part of Brian Clough's remarkable team of the late 1970s and early 1980s that went on to win the European Cup twice.

Anderson's debut came in a friendly against Czechoslovakia in 1978 and he went on to play 30 times for his country.

It was a great moment for the game in England and paved the way for over a hundred footballers with Black heritage playing for the Three Lions.

There is some debate as to whether Anderson was the first Black footballer to play for England. Previously, in 1968, Paul Reaney, the mixed-race Leeds United full back, had been selected.

PLAYER OF THE SEASON

At the end of the 2022–23 season the Arsenal winger, Bukayo Saka, 21 years old, was indisputably recognised as one of the top players in the Premier League, after his astonishing attacking ability had cut defences open and helped the north London club to come very close to being champions for the first time in 19 years.

But there is more to this story than a young player emerging as one of the greatest talents of his generation. Two years earlier Bukayo Saka had stepped up to take a penalty in the European Championships final at Wembley. He needed to score to keep England from losing the final on penalties to Italy.

He missed. England were defeated. And Saka received a torrent of racist abuse on social media. He was 19 at the time.

19 years old.

No-one should have to face this kind of hate. Saka was still a teenager, and had been called up to do something most of us wouldn't dare do. In front of hundreds of millions of people.

How he coped with the abuse we cannot imagine. But what we do know is that, two years later, he is held in such high esteem by fans of his and other clubs.

A great moment for him. A great moment for football.

APPLAUSE!!!!!!!!!

BUKAYO SAKA	
Born	2001, England
Position	Forward
Club goals	41
International goals	11
Selected honours	FA Cup; England Men's Player of the Year

INVINCIBLE

No team had ever done it before. And no team has done it since.

Since the formation of the Premier League, the champions each year have lost at least some of their games on their way to the title. Premier League champions have lost two, three, four, five, six and seven games. Chelsea had come the closest to avoiding defeat in 2003–04 when they lost only once.

But in 2003–04 Arsenal went a whole season without losing a single Premier League game. Home or away. Thus they were called the Invincibles. They won 26 of their 38 games and drew the other 12.

Even before the Premier League no champions had gone a whole season undefeated since Preston did it in 1888–89. Not even the great Liverpool teams of the 1970s and 1980s achieved this kind of invincibility...

Arsène Wenger's class of 2004, which included

legends Thierry Henry and Dennis Bergkamp, will remain forever undefeated, and indeed it is a feat that may never be repeated.

PREMIER LEAGUE 2003/4								
TEAM	Pl	W	D	L	F	A	GD	Pts
Arsenal	38	26	12	0	73	26	47	90
Chelsea	38	24	7	7	67	30	37	79
Manchester United	38	23	6	9	64	35	29	75
Liverpool	38	16	12	10	55	37	18	60

IT'S UP FOR GRABS NOW

In 1989, just three years before the Premier League was formed, the greatest ending to a top-flight English football season was played out at Anfield: Liverpool at home to Arsenal. It was the last game of the season, between the two teams who could still win the league. The table looked like this before the game:

	GAMES	FOR-AGAINST	GD	POINTS
Liverpool	37	65–26	+39	76
Arsenal	37	71–36	+35	73

To win the league, Arsenal needed to win by two clear goals. It was 0–0 at half time and it seemed the season would end with Liverpool crowned champions for the tenth time in 15 years. But on 53 minutes Alan Smith scored with a header.

One-nil to the Arsenal. They needed one more goal to be champions.

Time passed and before long the ninetieth minute came up on the clock. It was still 1–0. Both teams had had chances to score – but neither did. Still Liverpool champions. The officials began to prepare the trophy to present to the home team. But wait… Arsenal had time for one more attack.

Goalkeeper John Lukic bowled the ball to Lee Dixon. Dixon hit a long ball up to Alan Smith. Smith lofted the ball into the path of Michael Thomas. Thomas clipped the ball and it bounced back off the defender, Steve Nichol, to his feet. Now Thomas was in on goal. One touch. Two touches.

'It's up for grabs now…' the commentator shouted.

And Michael Thomas clipped the ball over Bruce Grobbelaar. 2–0.

GOALLLLLLLL!

The season was over. Arsenal were champions. Liverpool's era of almost complete dominance of the English game was over.

Arsenal won it on goals scored. With the last kick of the season.

	GAMES	FOR-AGAINST	GD	POINTS
Arsenal	38	73–37	+38	76
Liverpool	38	66–28	+38	76

CARLISLE 2 PLYMOUTH 1

Ten years later – at the end of the 1998–99 season –
a goal that stands alongside Michael Thomas's league
winner was scored at the bottom end of the league. A
goal even more bizarre.

It was scored in the fourth tier of English football,
90-odd places below the likes of Arsenal and
Liverpool. Carlisle United were drawing 1–1 with
Plymouth Argyle, but needed a win to avoid being
relegated out of the Football League and becoming a
non-league team in crisis.

With one minute of injury time to go and nothing
to lose, the Carlisle keeper, Jimmy Glass, joined nine
other outfield players cramming the box for a Carlisle
corner. He placed himself on the six-yard line, hoping
for a header.

Glass was not a Carlisle regular. He was playing
only his third game for the club, having been brought
in on loan from Swindon at the end of the season. He

would never play for them again. But for those three games – and for this one in particular – he would be remembered as a club legend.

Because Carlisle needed a goal. Or they were down and out. Literally.

The corner came across. A Carlisle attacker leaped and headed the ball hard toward the goal. The keeper, unable to hold such a hard shot, parried it and it fell onto the six-yard line.

To Jimmy Glass. Who side-footed it home and was then mobbed by his teammates.

UNBELIEVABLE!!!!!

After emerging from the melee, Glass saw the pitch had been invaded by hundreds of Carlisle fans, who joined him, patting his back, grinning with glee, as he ran back to his goal to play out the last seconds of the game.

NOISY NEIGHBOURS

When Manchester City evolved from a third-tier side in 1996–97 to potential English champions in 2012, the Manchester United manager, Sir Alex Ferguson, said that 'sometimes neighbours are noisy'.

That was never more true than in the last games of the 2011–12 season as United and City raced neck and neck to be champions.

City needed to equal United's result. So when United's game at Sunderland ended with the Reds as 1–0 winners they looked to see how their rivals were doing. At the Etihad the score was City 1, QPR 2 and heading into injury time. Naturally the United players and fans began to celebrate. Their team had won the Premier League eleven times since its formation 20 years earlier. It looked like it was about to be twelve. There was no way City could score twice in five minutes. Was there?

On 90+2 minutes Edin Džeko headed in to

equalise. There were two minutes of injury time to go, and only one goal needed.

The mood in both stadiums changed. Manchester United, nervy. Manchester City, urgent.

And then it happened. On 90+4 minutes, the ball broke to Sergio Agüero in the box. He took two touches and hit the ball so hard that the keeper could never have stopped it.

AGÜEROOOOOOOOOOOOOOOOOO!

The noise in the Etihad was so loud, it was heard loud and clear across the city at Old Trafford. Manchester City were the ultimate noisy neighbours.

PREMIER LEAGUE	
Sunday, 13 May 2012	
Manchester City 3–2 Queen's Park Rangers	
Pablo Zabaleta 39'	Djibril Cissé 48'
Edin Džeko 90+2'	Jamie Mackie 66'
Sergio Agüero 90+4''	

FIRST MINUTE

Last-minute goals are the ones that make history.
They bring drama, sudden and shocking shifts in
the history of the game of football. But in 1919, a
first-minute goal felt like it was about more than
the history of football. It was about the history of
the world.

Between 1914 and 1919, England men did not
play any full international football. There was a war
on. Young men were not playing football: they were
at war. A war in which 10 million young men died.

England kicked off their first official international
after the war in Belfast, playing Ireland. Playing at
centre forward was the former Huddersfield and now
Chelsea player, Jack Cock. A man who had fought
through most of the war and witnessed terrible
events and tragedies at the battle of the Somme and
Delville Wood, two of the most appalling battles in
human history.

Europe was full of young men like Jack, shattered by five years of fighting and fear. Young men who had survived. And young men who had not: killed or broken on the battlefields of Europe.

Jack must have been nervous as the game kicked off. He was making his debut as an England player after all that carnage.

He didn't show it. With his first touch he controlled the ball. With his second he scored. After 30 seconds.

He'd scored England's first goal after the end of the war. On his debut.

HOME CHAMPIONSHIPS	
Saturday, 19 August 2023	
Ireland 1–1 England	
Jimmy Ferris 70'	Jack Cock 1'

NOT SUITABLE

By the end of the First World War a million women were working in factories, engineering the shells and other munitions for the Army and the Navy needed to win the war. Women were doing jobs that were considered not suitable for women before the war.

It was exhausting work. It was dangerous work, with many women being killed or made very ill by explosions and the poisonous materials they handled to make the shells.

In their breaks and on their days off – to enjoy the little free time they had – the women of the factories, called munitionettes, played football.

Football was made for this moment in history. A sport played and watched by working people, to bring relief and joy and togetherness.

Soon different armament factories played each other. Tournaments were played, increasingly in the stadiums that were built for men to play a sport that – like engineering – was considered not suitable for women.

War had changed everything. Football was changing lives and challenging the absurd idea that women couldn't – or shouldn't – play football.

BOOOOOOOOOOOO!

BOXING DAY 1920

It was Boxing Day 1920. The terrible war was over and world was trying to live normally again. In Liverpool, the turnstiles were closed and fans were being turned away as Goodison Park was already full. Some 53,000 fans were inside to watch one of the great teams of the era. A team of footballers who worked in a factory called Dick, Kerr & Co.

Dick, Kerr Ladies. A munitionettes factory team from Preston. With one of the great footballers in the history of the game.

Lily Parr.

A tall, strong forward who was impossible to bully off the ball. Scorer of over 950 goals in a phenomenal career that began with 43 goals in her first full season, aged only 14.

The Boxing Day 1920 game was so successful, such a great moment in football, that men decided that the women's game was doing too well and was jeopardising the men's game's chances of recovery after the First World War.

So in 1921 men banned women playing football on FA grounds from parks to stadiums. Across the entire country.

The ban would last half a century.

That game on Boxing Day 1920 is remembered as one of the greatest moments in football. And, also, one of the most shameful.

LILY PARR	
Born	1905, England
Position	Forward
Club goals	967

HALF A CENTURY LATER

Is it right to call the lifting of the ban on women playing football as a one of the greatest moments in football?

You decide.

In one way – yes – it was a happy day that women were once again allowed to play football again, allowed to use facilities that had been reserved for men for 50 years. Stadiums. Pitches. Parks. Sport centres.

But – in another way – can we celebrate the half-century of sexism during which women were banned from playing a game? It seems ridiculous.

It is worth pointing out that the FA were forced to lift their ban by UEFA, Europe's football governing body. It wasn't their idea.

It is also worth pointing out that the FA did not actually fund the women's game for a further 22 years, not until 1993.

To be allowed to play football. Just think about that.

And women would even be *allowed* to use Wembley...

WEMBLEY 2022

It's 31 July 2022. Fifty million people are watching extra time in the European Championships 2022 final between England and Germany.

The score is 1–1. England win a corner. Lauren Hemp gathers the ball and prepares to loft it into the penalty area. The crowd is chanting, urging their team to get that one goal England need to win the Euros for the first time in history.

Chloe Kelly – a young forward from Man City – arrives in the box, lining up with several teammates against a wall of tall German defenders.

She takes a deep breath. Hemp swings the ball into the area. Three England players leap, and the ball drops among England and German boots inside the six-yard area.

To Kelly.

Kelly lashes at the ball, but it seems to come back off the keeper. Back to Kelly again. She stabs at the ball, retaining her balance.

The noise is impossible.

The ball has gone between the German keeper's legs.

GOOOOAAAAALLLLLLLL!

England 2, Germany 1.

Kelly and her teammates run ecstatically towards the England bench, Kelly waving her shirt above her head.

One of the two greatest moments in English football.

EUROPEAN CHAMPIONSHIP FINAL	
Sunday, 31 July 2022	
England 2–1 Germany	
Ella Toone 62'	Lina Magull 79'
Chloe Kelly 110'	

THEY THINK IT'S ALL OVER...

The other greatest moment in English football was the moment when the England men's team knew they had won their first major trophy (and still their only major trophy).

Wembley. 1966. The World Cup final.

England are leading the final 3–2 with one minute left. The England defence hoofs the ball up field to Geoff Hurst who has acres of space as West Germany press for an equaliser.

The words of the commentator Kenneth Wolstenholme were heard in millions of homes up and down the country:

And here comes Hurst...
Some people are on the pitch...
They think it's all over...

Geoff Hurst controls the ball and powers into the

box. Four touches. The German keeper comes out, careful to cover his far post, where he expects the Englishman to place it. Hurst slams the ball inside the top near post. Another goal.

It is now, shouts the commentator.

WORLD CUP FINAL			
Saturday, 30 July 1966			
England 4–2 West Germany			
Geoff Hurst	19'	Helmut Haller	13'
Martin Peters	78'	Wolfgang Weber	90'
Geoff Hurst	101'		
Geoff Hurst	120'		

HAT TRICK HEROES

England's 1966 World Cup win was all the more remarkable because that last goal by Geoff Hurst was the first time a player had scored a hat trick in a World Cup final. Three goals in the world's greatest game.

A surprisingly long list of players have scored two goals in the World Cup final. Pelé, as we know, in 1958. But also Gino Colaussi (Italy, 1938), Silvio Piola (Italy, 1938), Helmut Rahn (West Germany, 1954), Vavá (Brazil, 1958), Mario Kempes (Argentina, 1978), Zinedine Zidane (France, 1998), Ronaldo (Brazil, 2002) and Lionel Messi (Argentina, 2022). Scoring two goals in a men's World Cup final was not that unusual.

But it was only when Kylian Mbappé scored a hat trick for France in the 2022 World Cup final that anyone matched Hurst's feat. Sadly for Mbappé he still finished on the losing side.

But – for both Mbappé and Hurst – to score a hat

trick in the world's greatest game unquestionably counts as a great moment. For Hurst to do it – and collect a winners' medal, too – is certainly one of the greatest.

GEOFF HURST	
Born	1941, England
Position	Forward
Club goals	228
International goals	24
Selected honours	FA Cup; European Cup Winners' Cup; World Cup

THE DOG THAT FOUND
THE WORLD CUP

Ninety-nine of my Greatest Moments in Football
relate to humans. Only one to a dog.

When England were preparing to host the 1966
World Cup the trophy was put on display for the
public to see.

And was stolen.

For a week the world watched on as the famous
British police force scrambled to find it. But with
no success. It was embarrassing for the police, the
FA and the country. What would happen if it was
never found?

A week after the theft a man was taking his collie,
Pickles, for a walk. Pickles was sniffing around
the front wheel of a car when he found an object
wrapped in newspaper. Puzzled, the man picked the
mysterious object up and tore some of the newspaper
away. There, he saw the words Argentina and West
Germany, the two teams from the previous final.

Pickles had found the World Cup.

Pickles was invited to the World Cup win celebration and his owner was given a reward large enough to buy a house. The dog was also awarded a medal, was made dog of the year and had a blue plaque attached to the wall where he once lived.

WOOOOOF!

PICKLES	
Born	1962, England
Position	Dog
Breed	Collie
Selected honours	World Cup; Very Good Boy

JACK

Two of England's 1966 World Cup winning heroes were brothers. Jack Charlton was the older sibling. A towering and somewhat brutal defender.

Jack – who played all 762 of his club games for Leeds United – was the only one of the team that won the World Cup as a player who went on to manage a team in the World Cup finals. Twice.

He took the Republic of Ireland to two World Cups (1990 and 1994) and one European Championships (1988), reaching the knockout stages of the World Cup both times and including victories against England and Italy.

A small country with a population of three and a half million, Ireland had never qualified for a finals tournament before Charlton came. This was an astonishing achievement. Something they would not have achieved – most people would say – without the former Leeds United player.

Jack Charlton's time in Ireland was marked by becoming the first Englishman to be awarded the Freedom of the City of Dublin since 1854. The English have a history of interfering brutally in the politics of Ireland, so for Jack to be awarded such an honour was a truly remarkable thing.

JACK CHARLTON	
Born	1935, England
Position	Centre back
Club goals	70
International goals	6
Selected honours	Football League First Division; FA Cup; World Cup

BOBBY

Bobby Charlton – Jack's younger brother – tried his hand at management, but it didn't work out. But what he achieved as a club player must go down as one of the most remarkable football stories ever.

In 1958 the Manchester United team were known as the Busby Babes, partly after their manager, Sir Matt Busby, and partly because they were such a young group of players. They excelled in Europe. But one snowy night, they were flying home from an away tie when their aeroplane crashed on an icy runway in Munich. 23 of the 44 passengers were killed, including nine of the 17 players.

It was one of the darkest days in world football.

Bobby was one of only six players on board to ever play again. But play again he did: ten years later, in the 1968 European Cup final against Eusébio's Benfica.

Manchester United – still managed by Busby – reached the pinnacle of club football by winning 4–1

FOOTBALL'S GREATEST MOMENTS

and cementing themselves as one of the greatest sides in European football.

Bobby Charlton scored twice on that day and lifted the trophy as captain.

EUROPEAN CUP FINAL	
Wednesday, 29 May 1968	
Manchester United 4–1 Benfica	
Bobby Charlton 53'	Graça 79'
George Best 92'	
Brian Kidd 94'	
Bobby Charlton 99'	

SCOTLAND, WORLD CHAMPIONS

In April 1967, Scotland became World Champions.

They went to Wembley to play England in the Home Championships less than a year after England had won the World Cup. At this point England still remained undefeated since their victory. Both Bobby and Jack Charlton were in the England team.

Scotland lined up against the same eleven that had lifted the Jules Rimet trophy and – although both Bobby Charlton and Geoff Hurst scored for the home team – the Scots won 3–2.

So, arguably, they could, in spring 1967, call themselves World Champions.

Regardless of whether Scotland had an argument worth arguing, it was a time of huge success for the Scottish game. Six of the players in their team that day would be representing Celtic and Rangers in European finals in the following few weeks: Rangers finishing as runners-up to Bayern Munich

in the Cup Winners' Cup and Celtic winning the
European Cup.

HOME CHAMPIONSHIPS			
Saturday, 15 April 1967			
England 2–3 Scotland			
Jack Charlton	85'	Denis Law	28'
Geoff Hurst	89'	Bobby Lennox	79'
		Jim McCalliog	87'

LISBON LIONS

In 1967, when Celtic FC travelled to Lisbon for the final of the twelfth European Cup (now re-branded as the UEFA Champions League), its previous winners were listed as Real Madrid (6 wins), Inter Milan (2), Benfica (2) and AC Milan (1).

Celtic would play Inter Milan, winners of the trophy for two of the previous three years. They were managed by the legendary Helenio Herrara and had a team packed with the cream of Italian, Spanish and Brazilian talent

Against Celtic, eleven men who had been born within 30 miles of Glasgow.

Six minutes in, Inter won a penalty. And scored. At half time the score was 1–0 to the Italians. Mission impossible, surely, for Celtic FC of Glasgow? Italian teams were all about defence, about winning 1–0.

So, with nothing to lose, Celtic attacked, making chance after chance to score, but somehow not converting those chances into goals.

Relentless, they pounded the famous Italian defence... which cracked in the 62nd minute, and then broke again in the 83rd.

Celtic 2, Inter Milan 1.

That Celtic team have become known as the Lisbon Lions. The first British team to win the tournament. An English team had never yet reached the final.

EUROPEAN CUP FINAL	
Thursday, 25 May 1967	
Celtic 2–1 Inter Milan	
Tommy Gemmell 63'	Sandro Mazzola 7' (P)
Stevie Chalmers 84'	

SIX IN A ROW

It is common for one country's football teams to dominate the European Cup or Champions League, as we know it now. Spain have won it five times in a row, twice over. The first time: Real Madrid, 1956 to 1960. The second: Real Madrid and Barcelona, 2013 to 2018.

Between 1970 and 1973, the Dutch won it four times on the trot with Ajax and Feyenoord. Then, following on from that, Bayern Munich of Germany won it from 1974 to 1976. (Dubiously in 1975, for the record.)

But only one country has won the European Cup six times in a row. With teams from three cities:

1977	Liverpool
1978	Liverpool
1979	Nottingham Forest
1980	Nottingham Forest
1981	Liverpool
1982	Aston Villa

That country is England. So, when Aston Villa, not a traditionally big club in modern game, won in 1982, it became one of football's greatest moments.

REMONTADA

The Champions League is famous for dramatic finals. But also, drama in its semi-finals, quarter-finals and even in the Round of 16. Once the group stages are over and teams must knock each other out, anything can happen.

That brings us to *La Remontada*.

This Spanish word *remontada* means 'to climb', 'to soar', 'to turn around'. And all those concepts can be applied to what Barcelona achieved when playing PSG in the 2017 Champions League Round of 16.

In the first leg, PSG beat Barcelona 4–0. And that should have been it.

Even with two minutes to go in the second leg, Barça led 3–1 with goals from Luis Suárez, Layvin Kurzawa and Lionel Messi. But they still trailed 3–5 on aggregate.

Then Neymar took a free kick in the 88th

minute. And scored. Now it was 4–1 – and 4–5 on aggregate.

Then a penalty on 90+1 minutes: 5–1 and 5–5 on aggregate. But PSG – with one goal scored in the Camp Nou – still led on away goals scored.

Could it happen?

On 90+5, Neymar gathered a clearance from another free kick. He dropped his shoulder, powered towards the penalty box, then lofted the ball.

Sergi Roberto stretched a leg forward and pushed the ball over the line.

And it was in.

Goal.

The result: 6–1 on the night, 6–5 on aggregate. Barcelona had climbed and soared and turned the game around.

LA REMMMMMMMMONTADAAAAAAAAA!

FERGIE TIME

But which is the ultimate comeback in English football's Champions' League history?

There is no debate that Manchester United's Champions' League win in 1999 and Liverpool's win in 2005 are two of the greatest moments in football. But which is the more dramatic? Which is the greater moment of the two?

In the 1999 Champions' League final, Man U are losing 1–0 to Bayern Munich. The 90 minutes are up. The referee has allotted three minutes for injury time.

But everyone knows you must never dismiss Man U until the final whistle. Sometimes the Reds get so much injury time it is referred to as Fergie Time, after their clock-watching manager on the bench, Sir Alex Ferguson.

One minute into Fergie time, United pile forward. Peter Schmeichel is out of his goal to add to the numbers, trying to scrape an equaliser and force

extra time. The ball is hoofed clear by the Germans.
To Ryan Giggs who scuffs a poor shot. Not at goal.
It spins towards the substitute, Teddy Sheringham.
Unmarked. Almost unready. But he steadies himself
and sweeps it home.

It's 1–1, all square. The noise is deafening. Man U
have done it again in injury time.

But there's more. Still more Fergie time.

At 90+3, Man U win a corner. David Beckham
wastes no time and lofts the ball into the box.
Sheringham is there again. He catches it with his
head, but the ball drops towards the goal line between
German keeping legend Oliver Kahn and another
Man U substitute, Ole Gunnar Solskjær.

The Norwegian moves first and lifts the ball into
the net. 2–1.

GOOOAALLLLLLL!!!!

An unbelievable comeback.

'And nobody will ever win a European
cup final more dramatically than this!' the
commentator screams.

YOU'LL NEVER WALK ALONE

When you walk through the crowd at the Ataturk Stadium in Istanbul, Turkey, you hold your head up high. You made it! You saved all the money you could so you could see your team, Liverpool, in the Champions' League final.

With 1,700 miles travelled and hundreds of pounds spent, you have hope in your heart. But then you're losing 3–0 at half time. Your dreams are tossed and blown. But you are about to witness history.

They call it the Miracle of Istanbul. The legend is that it began with the fans. As the players emerge for the second half you start to sing your anthem. And now thousands of other Liverpool fans have joined in.

Walk on! Walk on!
With hope in your heart
And you'll never walk alone.
You'll neeeeeeeever walk alone.

The miracle pours from the terraces. From the fans to the players.

Steven Gerrard scores. It's 3–1. Louder now. You hold your head up high.

Vladimir Šmicer scores. It's 3–2. Louder still. There's a golden sky.

Then Xabi Alonso. It's 3–3. All square. Extra time, then penalties.

And victory.

It's a miracle. Born of a song.

CHAMPIONS LEAGUE	
Wednesday, 25 May 2005	
Milan 3–3 Liverpool	
Paolo Maldini 1'	Steven Gerrard 54'
Hernán Crespo 39'	Vladimir Šmicer 56'
Hernán Crespo 44'	Xabi Alonso 61'
Liverpool won 3–2 on penalties	

"NESSUN DORMA"

With Italy hosting the 1990 World Cup, the BBC had to choose some music to lead into their programmes. They chose 'Nessun Dorma' ('Let No One Sleep'), from Puccini's opera *Turandot*, and sung in this version by the Italian operatic tenor, Luciano Pavarotti.

A slow quiet voice and gentle music builds and builds towards a powerful performance from Pavarotti. If you play it to any football lover over the age of 40, it is very likely the hairs on their arms will go up and they'll smile. Pavarotti's version even entered the pop singles chart in the UK, reaching number two.

Music and sport inextricably linked. A tournament that few who watched it will forget.

Germany beat Argentina in the final. England's fourth placing was their closest to winning the cup since 1966. A remarkable Italian called Salvatore Schillaci was the tournament's leading scorer.

But – even though Pavarotti was a consummate performer – a young English footballer called Gazza stole the show.

And England won the fair play trophy.

NESSSSSSSSUN DORMAAAAAAA!

PAUL GASCOIGNE	
Born	1967, England
Position	Attacking midfielder
Club goals	83
International goals	10
Selected honours	FA Cup; Scottish Premier Division; Scottish Cup; Scottish League Cup

TEARS

Italia '90. For the first time in a quarter of a century, England have a team that could win the World Cup, with 'Nessun Dorma' ringing in their ears. There's a spirit. With players like Chris Waddle and Gary Lineker, Stuart Pearce and the 100+ cap goalkeeper Peter Shilton.

But the player who is capable of winning the World Cup for England, if they can do that, is a young player called Paul Gascoigne. Gazza for short. His genius, creativity and unpredictability on the pitch is important. But so is his mischief-making around the hotel pool, having fun and breaking the tournament tension among his teammates. With Gazza, England have a chance. The youngster just has to avoid picking up a second booking in the semi-final against Germany.

It's 1–1 in the semi-final in Turin, the home of Juventus. In extra time and heading for penalties.

Gazza is weaving though the Germans again, the ball at his feet. But, as it runs away from him, he tackles Thomas Berthold clumsily in an attempt to win it back.

Gazza goes to apologise to the German, not wanting to catch the referee's eye. He had that feeling when you know something bad might happen.

Which it does.

The referee brandishes a yellow card, and the English fans know that even if their team can reach the World Cup final, Gazza now cannot. Gazza walks away from the foul, from his teammates. Gary Lineker goes to comfort him, but the young Geordie is staring into the distance. He is in tears. Broken.

And, with Gazza's head gone, England's chance is gone too. They lose the penalty shoot-out.

IT'S COMING HOME

It is six years after Italia '90 and England are hosting Euro '96, the first major men's tournament to be held in England since 1966. Expectations are high. Three group games at Wembley. *It's coming home.*

But it's also tense. The expectation of success seems almost like a weight on the shoulders of the England players. Even though all their games are at their home ground. And England have been disappointing in their opening game against Switzerland, a mere draw.

They are now 1–0 up against Scotland. But Scotland, are close to equalising as the Swiss did. Gary McAllister has just missed a penalty. The crowd are anxious. The players, too. England need to score. England have to win this game. Their last group game will be against the Dutch, one of the best teams in the world.

There is that sense that it could all go wrong.

Until the ball breaks for Gazza. He runs onto it,

with the defender, Colin Hendry, blocking the goal.
So Gazza lifts it over Hendry. The defender falls. And,
before the ball touches the turf, Gazza volleys it past
the helpless Scotland keeper.

Wembley erupts. England 2, Scotland 0 with just
ten minutes left. Confidence floods the stadium.
Even more excitingly, England go on to beat the
Netherlands 4–1 in the next game, reaching the
knockout stages.

Thanks to Gazza's magical strike.

EUROPEAN CHAMPIONSHIPS GROUP A	
Saturday, 15 June 1996	
Scotland 0–2 England	
	Alan Shearer 53'
	Paul Gascoigne 79'

SCOTLAND IN DREAMLAND

Argentina 1978. Scotland are carrying home nation hopes in the World Cup finals as the only team from the British Isles to qualify.

But their first two group games have been a disappointment: a 3–1 defeat to Peru followed by a 1–1 draw with Iran. And now they have to face the best team in Europe – the Netherlands – and beat them by three goals. It's an unlikely outcome, but in football, the unlikely is always possible.

With only a few minutes to go it is hard to believe Scotland are 2–1 up. A small, balding figure picks up a loose ball on the edge of the Dutch penalty area.

Gemmill, says the commentator.

Archie Gemmill, midfielder for the English league champions, Nottingham Forest, controls the ball, weaves past two orange shirts and breaks into the box.

Good play by Gemmill. And again.

Another player beaten. And another. Gemmill is in

on goal, switches feet and – with his left – shoots.

Three-one! A brilliant individual goal by this hard little professional has put Scotland in dreamland. They need one more to qualify.

One more goal to put the best team out of the World Cup and qualify for the knockout stages.

And one more goal came. But it was for the Netherlands. And Scotland's dream was over.

WORLD CUP GROUP D			
Sunday, 11 June 1978			
Scotland 3–2 Netherlands			
Kenny Dalglish	45'	Ron Rensenbrink	35' (P)
Archie Gemmill	47' (P)	Johnny Rep	72'
Archie Gemmill	68'		

BALE'S WALES TALES

Wales had not qualified for a World Cup or European Championship since 1958 when they lost in the quarter-final against Brazil featuring a teenage Pelé. But 58 years later they reached Euro 2016, a tournament for which Belgium were firm favourites.

And it was Belgium that Wales – featuring their world-class forward, Gareth Bale – were to face in only the second quarter-finals in their history, having already seen off Slovakia, Russia and Northern Ireland in the tournament.Though they had lost in injury time to England, Wales still topped the group above their noisy neighbours.

But England were out – defeated by an even noisier Iceland – and now Wales had to face a Belgium team featuring Thibaut Courtois, Eden Hazard, Romelu Lukaku, Kevin De Bruyne and Marouane Fellaini. With a victory Wales 2016 would go one better than Wales 1958 and reach a major semi-final for the first time in their history.

The toughest of challenges. A European football giant against a country with a population of only three million. Wales needed a miracle.

But miracles happen.

With goals from Ashley Williams, Hal Robson-Kanu and Sam Vokes they shocked the Belgian golden generation and Wales became the first British team to reach a major semi-final for 20 years.

EUROPEAN CHAMPIONSHIPS QF			
Friday, 1 July 2016			
Wales 3–1 Belgium			
Ashley Williams	30'	Radja Nainggolan	13'
Hal Robson-Kanu	55'		
Sam Vokes	85'		

TO SPAIN TO SHOW THEM HOW TO PLAY THE GAME

When Northern Ireland – with a population of one million – qualified for the Spain 1982 World Cup they recorded a song with popular singer, Dana. In the song they claimed they'd 'go to Spain' and 'show them how to play the game'.

A nice rhyme. But quite a claim.

The Spanish team will have been looking forward to meeting Northern Ireland in their last group game, having beaten Yugoslavia and drawn with Honduras. Northern Ireland had drawn with both and were the lowest-ranked side in the group. Spain would win and go on to the next stages of the World Cup. Northern Ireland would go home. That was the plan.

The key moment came just after half-time. Spain were knocking the ball about, controlling possession, displaying a style of elegant play which was a hallmark of so many successful Spanish teams down the years.

But then one of their many passes went astray and

centre-forward Gerry Armstrong – forced to play deep to get his feet on the ball – took it and ran hard. He powered for 50 yards with the ball at his feet, then laid it wide to Billy Hamilton on the right. With Spain stretched, Hamilton managed to beat one defender and get a cross in. Panicking, the keeper pushed the ball out towards the penalty spot.

Gerry Armstrong arrived just in time, breathless after his length-of-the-pitch run, to hammer the ball home. Low and hard through the keeper and defender. Unstoppable.

Spain 0, Northern Ireland 1. Enough for both teams to qualify for the next stage. Lesson learned.

THE GREATEST GAME
OF FOOTBALL

Italy's clash with Brazil in the 1982 World Cup finals is considered by some to be the greatest game of football ever played.

It was a meeting of the two dominant football cultures: Brazil's attacking game characterised by passing, possession and fluid football, versus Italy's more defensive, counter-attacking style.

Over the four games before they met Brazil had scored a total of twelve goals in the tournament, averaging three goals a game. Italy meanwhile had amassed a total of just four, averaging one goal per game. And with free-scoring players like Zico, Socrates and Falcao on form, Brazil were favourites to win the game and the tournament, against an Italy whose striker, Paolo Rossi had failed to score, drawing calls from home for him to be dropped.

But Rossi played, scoring after five minutes. Brazil equalised after twelve.

Rossi scored again after 25 minutes, stealing the ball off the South Americans as they passed it about in their easy style, then slamming it home. Then, in the 68th minute, Brazil equalised again.

Now, with the game at 2–2 and with the Brazilians pressing for a winner to prove their flairsome football was the way to play the game, Rossi scored a third. His hat trick.

The unthinkable had happened: 3–2. Italy had won; Brazil were out. And Rossi and his teammates went on to win the World Cup.

WORLD CUP GROUP C	
Monday, 5 July 1982	
Italy 3–2 Brazil	
Paolo Rossi 5'	Sócrates 12'
Paolo Rossi 25'	Falcão 68'
Paolo Rossi 74'	

FRANCE 1998

France was the country that had invented the World Cup, the original trophy in 1930 being named after its founder, Jules Rimet. And, yet, as they prepared to host the 1998 tournament, their national team had never won it in its 68-year history.

France had even hosted the tournament once before, in 1938. But Italy won it in Paris as war clouds gathered over Europe.

Fast forward to 1998. The sky darkening over Paris. France faced favourites, Brazil, in the final. But France had Zinedine Zidane, a man destined to become France's greatest footballer, in part for his two magnificent headers in the match.

Both headers came from corners and both were headed with such power and accuracy that no keeper would have stopped them.

It was a great moment for Zidane, for the French football team and for France as a nation. The celebrations went on for days. The French had achieved their destiny.

Emanuel Petit scored a third goal with the last kick of the game and France won 3–0 even though Marcus Desailly was sent off with 22 minutes to go.

But Desailly would not be the last player to be sent off in a World Cup final for France.

WORLD CUP FINAL	
Sunday, 12 July 1998	
France 3–0 Brazil	
Zinedine Zidane 27'	
Zinedine Zidane 45+1'	
Emmanuel Petit 90+3'	

ZIDANE'S CAREER ENDS IN DISGRACE

The greatest footballer to represent France was the attacking midfielder Zinedine Zidane. He had scored twice to win the 1998 World Cup for his country, had won countless trophies and awards with Bordeaux, Juventus and Real Madrid, and had won 108 caps for his country. His final game in blue was his second World Cup final, France versus Italy, in 2006.

It was tight with two early goals, and Zidane, captaining his country, opened the scoring after seven minutes. Italy's Marco Materazzi equalised after 19. The score was 1–1 after 90 minutes and remained so for a further 20.

In the 110th minute the two scorers – Zidane and Materazzi – were seen talking during a break in play. Talking and jostling. Suddenly Zidane took a step back, then charged to headbutt Materazzi in the chest. The Italian went flying.

After some confusion the Frenchman was sent off.

As he walked, the TV commentator John Motson announced, 'Zidane's career ends in disgrace.'

Zidane went on to win the award for player of that World Cup tournament, and went on to a superb managerial career, winning the Champions' League three years on the trot at Real Madrid.

But although Italy won the 2006 World Cup final on penalties, it is Zidane's last act as a French international that is now best remembered.

ZINEDINE ZIDANE	
Born	1972, France
Position	Attacking midfielder
Club goals	95
International goals	31
Selected honours	Serie A (2 times); La Liga; Champions League; World Cup

HOW TO PERFORM THE CRUYFF TURN

A defender is between you and the goal. You haven't been able to beat her once during the game. You need to deploy the Cruyff Turn.

First, take control of the ball, then turn your back on the defender. Next, feint to play the ball to your left or run to the left with the ball.

Now, lift your foot over the top of the ball, then drag your foot and the ball back to the right, turning your body to go the right as your adversary's weight moves to the left.

Now you have a clear path at goal, the defender left in your wake.

One of the most skilful footballers ever to play the game – the Dutch legend, Johan Cruyff – performed this skill notably during the 1974 World Cup. His first use of the move on the world stage was when the Netherlands played Sweden in a group game. It was so remarkable, and he performed it so effectively, that it became known as the Cruyff Turn. Probably the most famous single skill performed in the history of football and, therefore, one of football's greatest moments.

WOWWWWW!

JOHAN CRUYFF	
Born	1947, Netherlands
Position	Forward
Club goals	294
International goals	33
Selected honours	Eredivisie (9 times); La Liga; European Cup (3 times)

WE'VE GOT OUR BICYCLES BACK

After the Euro '88 semi-final, when the Netherlands beat West Germany 2–1 on German soil, almost 60 per cent of the Dutch population went out onto the streets of Amsterdam and in other cities to celebrate, many chanting an unusual song.

About bicycles.

The semi-final was the first time the Netherlands had beaten the Germans in a competitive fixture for 43 years, the first such win since the end of the Second World War.

Nazi Germany occupied the Netherlands from May 1940 to May 1945. It was brutal. The Nazis murdered 107,000 Dutch people as part of the Holocaust and – by taking away much of the Dutch food – starved another 18,000 people to death in their own country. Altogether 205,901 children, women and men died because of the war.

Among the lesser crimes the Germans committed

was to steal most of the Dutch people's bicycles. Firstly, while the occupation was ongoing; secondly, for many German soldiers to retreat after defeat by the Allies.

And that is why – overwhelmed with emotions that came as a shock to many of them – a country sang 'We've got our bicycles back', over and over into the night.

BICYCLES BACK... BICYCLES BACK... WE GOT OUR BICYCLES BACK!

EUROPEAN CHAMPIONSHIPS SF	
Tuesday, 21 June 1988	
West Germany 1–2 Netherlands	
Lothar Matthäus 55'	Ronald Koeman 74'
	Marco Van Basten 88'

HAND OF GOD

The 1982 war between Argentina and the UK, over who had the right to call the Falkland Islands theirs, had been a terrible conflict that led to the deaths of 904 soldiers, sailors and airmen, and much suffering on both sides.

Four years later, at the World Cup finals in Mexico, tensions lingered as Argentina and England faced each other in the quarter-finals. Shortly after half-time, Diego Maradona – then indisputably the best player in the world – leaped to head a ball into the net. Being a small man, Maradona was unable to reach the ball with his head, so he used his hand to knock the ball over England keeper, Peter Shilton.

Immediately Shilton and the other England players protested to the referee. Even the Argentina players didn't celebrate, until Maradona insisted that they hug him, fearful the referee would not allow the goal.

Without having seen the handball and without a

Video Assistant Referee to rely on – VAR would not come into use in the World Cup finals for another 32 years – the goal stood.

After the game Diego Maradona suggested the goal had, in fact, been scored by the hand of God. He also declared that it was symbolic revenge for Argentina's defeat in the 1982 war.

Thus, most Argentina fans would see the Hand of God as one of the greatest moments in football – but most English fans don't see it that way.

CHEAT! CHEAT! CHEAT!

WORLD CUP QF	
Sunday, 22 June 1986	
Argentina 2–1 England	
Diego Maradona 51'	Gary Lineker 81'
Diego Maradona 55'	

FEET OF GOD

Having only just been shattered by the injustice of conceding to the Hand of God in the 51st minute of the 1986 World Cup quarter-final, England were again beaten by Maradona in the 55th minute.

It meant a two-goal lead that England would not come back from.

This time the goal was not outrageous because of cheating and blasphemy, but outrageous on account of the breathtaking skill of the world's greatest footballer.

The ball came to Maradona in his own half of the pitch. Covered by two England players, he appeared to perform two Cruyff turns, creating the space to power through the summer heat, running 68 metres in eleven seconds, with eleven touches, never losing control, until he drew Shilton off his line and slotted the ball home.

It was the best goal many had ever seen. With such sublime footwork it became referred to as the 'Feet of God' – to complement the 'Hand of God' – and showed the two sides of a football player whose life on and off the pitch was forever controversial.

DIEGO MARADONA	
Born	1960, Argentina
Position	Attacking midfielder
Club goals	259
International goals	34
Selected honours	Serie A (2 times); World Cup; FIFA Player of the Century

DRAGBACK

Back in 1953, England had never lost at home to a team from outside the British Isles – and didn't expect to. The English had invented the game and considered themselves untouchable. They had only bothered to enter the World Cup once since its inception.

When Hungary arrived in England as Olympic Champions in 1953, few people really knew much about their team, or their star player Ferenc Puskás. A future England manager, Bobby Robson, would admit years later that he knew so little about the Hungarians they might as well have come from Mars.

The game began badly, England conceding within a minute. Very soon it became obvious that England were being outclassed and outplayed and were tactically naïve.

The game finished England 3, Hungary 6, and was notable for a remarkable dragback, when Ferenc Puskás, on the six-yard line, drew his defender into a tackle, pulled the ball back to leave the defender on the grass and, now in plenty of space, slotted the ball home. The move seemed to symbolise how out of touch English football was with the modern game.

The dragback and the result were a humiliation for the England team, but not as humiliating as the match in Hungary a year later, when England lost 7–1.

England football changed from that day on, with future legendary managers of the game such as Alf Ramsey, Matt Busby and Don Revie educating themselves in the tactics of teams across Europe.

Not a great day for England, but surely one of the greatest moments in football.

FERENC PUSKÁS	
Born	1927, Hungary
Position	Forward
Club goals	514
International goals	84
Selected honours	La Liga (5 times); European Cup (3 times)

THE SCORPION KICK

In 1995, 42 years after Puskás's dragback of the ball, another international player performed a remarkable trick in the same penalty area at Wembley.

This time it was Colombia's René Higuita.

Known as the master of the unpredictable – or as *el loco* (the madman) – Higuita waited for a looping Jamie Redknapp shot to arrive and – rather than catching it easily, as he could have – shocked Wembley by diving forwards, lifting his legs behind himself and volleying the ball back into play with his heels.

The move became known as the scorpion kick, as Higuita's body made the shape of a scorpion. And although the game and Redknapp's shot were inconsequential, the game being a friendly, Higuita's unconventional save stands as one of the most remarkable football plays ever seen at Wembley or across the world.

THE SAVE

In 1970 Brazil were the best football team in the
world. They also had the best player in the world: Pelé.

So, when Brazil tore down England's right in
that year's World Cup final group stage match and
Jairzinho's cross sailed over two England defenders
onto the head of Pelé, and when Pelé headed it
perfectly into the ground, so that the ball bounced
back up and toward the net, even Pelé himself
shouted goal.

GOALLLLLLLLLLLLLLL—

But it was not to be.

Somehow England keeper, Gordon Banks, had
tracked the ball, got a hand to it, and had forced the
ball to spin over the cross bar and bounce behind
the goal.

A save. Not a goal.

Pelé said later that it was the best save he had
ever seen.

KEEPER

Football is a game of such drama and stories that most books and films that try to tell stories about the game never make it over the line.

But in 2003 the English children's author, Mal Peet, published *Keeper*.

Keeper is the story of a South American international goalkeeper and his story leading up to winning the World Cup. Set in an unnamed country that feels much like Brazil, it features rainforests and ghosts, and the book would inspire a generation of other children's authors to write from the heart about the beautiful game.

It probably helped Mal Peet that he was writing about South America, the home of creativity in football.

BANANA KICK

It is a Brazilian who is credited with scoring the greatest free kick taken in the long story of football. His name is Roberto Carlos.

Playing in a friendly tournament in the lead up to the 1998 World Cup in France, Brazil won a free kick 35 yards out. Most teams would have decided to loft the ball into the penalty area from such a distance, hoping for a header into the goal, but Roberto Carlos wanted to go direct.

He placed the ball gently, then turned it over and over in his hands as it sat on the turf, appearing to study each panel of the ball. Next, he walked back 20 yards, stopping only when he reached the centre circle. The whistle blew and the Brazilian left back ran at the ball, a dozen steps, faster and faster, until he struck it ferociously with his right boot.

At first the ball appeared to be spinning wide. His teammates, the defensive wall and the French keeper,

Fabien Barthez, watched without moving, expecting a goal kick restart. And then the ball – moving at such speed – curved back on itself, smashing against the inside of the right-hand post, while the two teams stood like statues.

Goal. The ball had gone in.

The most remarkable free kick ever seen, it was immediately christened the Banana Kick.

ROBERTO CARLOS	
Born	1973, Brazil
Position	Left-back
Club goals	69
International goals	11
Selected honours	La Liga (4 times); Champion's League (3 times); World Cup

THE PANENKA

It's the final of the 1976 men's European Championships. The world champions West Germany versus Czechoslovakia. After extra time, it's 2–2 and for the first time a major football international tournament has to be decided by penalties.

The first seven penalties are scored, but then Germany miss. Meaning that Antonin Panenka, the Czech midfielder, can win the European Championships for his country if he scores his penalty.

Facing the legendary German keeper, Sepp Maier, Panenka steps up.

Imagine you're a keeper. You have to decide which way to dive. You can analyse the other player's form. You can consult your teammates. You can study the player's eyes and body language. But you have to choose which way to go. Left or right?

Panenka relied on the keeper doing that – going left or right – and coolly chipped the ball into the middle of the net, where the keeper had been standing a second before.

He scored. Czechoslovakia won the penalty shoot-out and the 1976 European Championships.

In years to come the technique would be copied by Zidane, Messi and Zlatan Ibrahimović. But it would always be known as the Panenka.

EUROPEAN CHAMPIONSHIP FINAL	
Sunday, 20 June 1976	
Czechoslovakia 2–2 West Germany	
Ján Švehlík 8'	Dieter Müller 28'
Karol Dobiaš 25'	Bernd Hölzenbein 89'
Czechoslovakia won 5–3 on penalties	

THE PENALTY

In the early days of football those involved were unsure what to do when a player was clearly prevented from scoring by foul play within 12 yards of the goal. A handball by an outfield player, for example, stopping the ball going over the line. Or a foul tackle. It was common for opposition players to do whatever they could to stop a goal, provided it was within the laws of the game.

The problem was there were so few laws back in the 1800s.

The first attempt to solve the problem was to award an indirect free kick to the fouled-against team. But this did nothing to prevent handballs and fouls as it remained a better option than conceding a goal.

The second idea for a solution was to simply award a goal if a foul or a handball was seen to prevent a certain goal. A little like the penalty try in rugby. But this idea lasted only one season.

The problem was solved by William McCrum, an Irish goalkeeper who, uneasy about seeing goals prevented by foul play, proposed a kick from 12 yards – one player kicking against the goalkeeper – as the fairest and kindest way of solving the problem.

Though penalties would never be seen as kind by those who suffered from the dreaded penalty miss.

FAILURE IS NOT
TAKING A PENALTY

To beat Spain in the quarter-final of Euro '96, England needed to win a penalty shoot-out. But England were renowned for failing to win on penalties, most famously in the World Cup semi-final against Germany at Italia '90.

When players were asked to volunteer to take a spot kick against Spain, Stuart Pearce volunteered immediately. As one of the two players who had missed in 1990, leading to England not reaching that year's World Cup final, the England manager, Terry Venables, asked him, 'Are you sure?'

Stuart Pearce was sure.

In an interview afterwards, asking why he had volunteered to take the kick, and was he not afraid of failing to score again, Pearce explained that 'failure is not taking a penalty'.

If you watch Stuart Pearce after that penalty against Spain goes in, the keeper unable to reach it due to its power and accuracy, you'll see him punch the air, shout into the crowd, punch the air again, then turn to the TV camera recording him, his face defiant.

COME ON!!!!!!!!!!!!!!!!!!!!!!!!!!!!

STUART PEARCE	
Born	1962, England
Position	Left-back
Club goals	82
International goals	5
Selected honours	Football League Cup (2 times); Football League First Division

ROLE MODEL

It was the first women's World Cup to be decided
by penalties. The USA versus China, played in the
Californian sun. 1999.

A tight tense game ended 0–0 after 90 minutes and
was still level after extra time.

And so: penalties.

When the final penalty taker stepped up, the score
was four each, China having missed one. This meant
that Brandi Chastain – in her home state and home
nation – had the chance to win the World Cup for the
USA with her kick.

Chastain stepped up, hit it hard and buried it in the
back of the net. USA had won the World Cup.

What Chastain did next became an iconic moment
for women athletes. She took off her football shirt and
waved it over her head.

Her celebration was copied by England's Chloe
Kelly, when she scored the winner in the Euro '22

final at Wembley against Germany. Chastain had become a role model for Kelly and for millions of other women and girls keen to celebrate sporting glory.

BRANDI CHASTAIN	
Born	1968, USA
Positions	Defender, midfielder
Club goals	7
International goals	30
Selected honours	World Cup (2 times); Olympic gold medal (2 times)

HALFWAY

The USA hadn't won the Women's World Cup for
16 years – not since Chastain's penalty – when they
reached the 2015 final against reigning champions
Japan. But 16 minutes after kick-off the game was all
but over: USA led 3–0.

Remarkably, all three USA goals had been scored
by forward Carli Lloyd. The first from a corner. The
second also from a corner. Both instinctive strikes
from inside the penalty area.

But the third goal was different. Picking the ball up
in her own half, Lloyd noticed the Japan keeper off the
line and, with one foot on the centre line, she hit a
powerful shot that sailed over the Japan defence, and
also over the flailing arms of the keeper.

A hat trick for Lloyd. The first in a World Cup final
since Geoff Hurst in 1966. Completed in the first 13
minutes in the biggest game at the highest level.

But one game doesn't define a player. Lloyd's other

achievements were 316 caps for her country, during which she scored 134 goals, as well as being named the FIFA World Player of the Year in 2016.

CARLI LLOYD	
Born	1982, USA
Positions	Midfielder, forward
Club goals	78
International goals	134
Selected honours	World Cup (2 times); Olympic gold medal (2 times)

THE KINGS OF FOOTBALL

The USA have a history of sometimes shocking the world of football. That began in the 1950 World Cup finals, held in Brazil.

The shock occurred against England. England were clear favourites, having recently beaten Italy 4–0, to whom the USA had lost 7–1.

In their first game the USA had been soundly beaten by Spain. England had beaten Chile 2–0, fielding legends of the early English game, like Stan Mortenson, Billy Wright and Tom Finney. Now the United States of America had to play the so-called Kings of Football. Defeat against their former colonial masters would see them out of the World Cup with a game to go.

The rest, though, is history. The game finished 1–0 to the USA and a new Republic of Football was born.

KILLING GIANTS IN MIDDLESBROUGH

The next great giant-killing in the men's World Cup was inflicted in 1966 on Italy at Middlesbrough's stadium, Ayresome Park – hundreds of miles away from the glamour of Wembley Stadium in London, where England were winning all their games to finish as World Cup Champions.

Italy's defeat came against a country that was still reeling from a brutal war in the previous decade. In fact, North Korea was not even recognised as a real country by governments in Europe at the time. But that was politics. It was football that mattered in Middlesbrough.

In football, Italy were twice world champions and in 1966 boasted players from Inter Milan, winners of the 1964 and 1965 European Cups.

But the final score was Italy 0 North Korea 1.

In winning, North Korea became the first team from outside Europe or South America to qualify for the knockout stages of a men's World Cup finals.

They looked set to kill another giant, Portugal, in the quarter-finals of the 1966 tournament, leading 3–0 after 25 minutes. But it was Eusébio's Portugal they were up against, and the great man scored four goals in 32 minutes to turn the game on its head, Portugal going on to win 5–3.

The greatest giant-killing of the World Cup so far was already in the history books. The North Koreans would return home as heroes. The Italians were pelted with tomatoes.

WORLD CUP GROUP 4	
Tuesday, 19 July 1966	
North Korea 1–0 Italy	
Doo Pak 43'	

NAÏVE

When Italia '90 kicked off, the World Cup holders, Argentina, were drawn to play Cameroon in the first game. That is the tradition: the winners of the previous World Cup open the next tournament, to get things off to an exciting start.

There was much enthusiasm for African teams in 1990. But one thing that was frequently said about them was that they were 'naïve'. Suggesting they were tactically inferior.

And so everyone expected the World Cup holders, Argentina – led by Diego Maradona – to win easily. When the referee sent off a Cameroon player early in the second half, that seemed even more likely.

But after 67 minutes a ball spun up, deflected into the Argentina penalty area. In just two seconds of disarray, the experienced Argentina defence left Cameroon's François Omam-Biyik completely unmarked, giving him acres of space to head the ball through the hands of the fumbling South American keeper.

Cameroon had taken the lead: 1–0. Even after a second of their players was given a red card, the remaining nine-man Cameroon team held out and shocked the world.

They went on to beat Romania and Colombia, and become the first team from Africa to reach the quarter-finals of the World Cup, where they were extremely unlucky to lose to England.

Hardly 'naïve'.

WORLD CUP GROUP B
Friday, 8 June 1990
Argentina 0–1 Cameroon
François Omam-Biyik   68'

GREAT GOAL, MR PRESIDENT

One of the many African players to become a legend in European football was the Liberian, George Weah. An exceptional attacker, he won major trophies in France, Italy and England.

He is best remembered as a player for his time at AC Milan: his box-to-box powerful attacking runs, his devastating finishes and what remains, for many, his greatest goal.

Serie A, 1996. Verona come to the San Siro. There's a corner. To the visitors. They over-hit it and Weah collects it inside his own penalty area. Then he turns and runs.

Hard and fast, he dodges half a dozen tackles before breaking into the Verona half of the field. As he approaches the goal, he has five yellow shirts chasing him in his iconic Milan red and black stripes. None will catch him.

Weah draws the keeper and fires it past him. He is

FIFA World Player of the Year. He is the holder of the Ballon d'Or, the second African to achieve this. On the pitch he is untouchable. It is an exceptional goal.

Off the pitch – after 488 games and 212 goals – he retired, went into politics and became the president of Liberia.

GEORGE WEAH	
Born	1966, Liberia
Position	Forward
Club goals	194
International goals	18
Selected honours	Ligue 1; Serie A (2 times); FA Cup

THE FIRST

The first African to win the Ballon d'Or was the Portugal international, Eusébio.

Eusébio was born in the south-east African country, Mozambique, but on moving to Portugal took dual citizenship and would become celebrated as one of the best players in history.

He lives on in the memory of those who saw him play, and could boast some outrageous statistics: 41 goals for Portugal in 64 games; 317 goals for Benfica in 301 games, including his contribution to his team's winning the 1962 European Cup.

His greatest moment came in 1965, when he became the first African to win the Ballon d'Or. To presented with the ultimate individual player award in Europe – at a time that players such as Ferenc Puskás, Bobby Charlton, Lev Yashin and Franz Beckenbauer were at their height of their powers – was a remarkable achievement.

Although Eusébio won the Ballon d'Or as a Portugal player, he kept dual citizenship and spent his later years setting up several charities in his home country of Mozambique.

EUSÉBIO	
Born	1942, Mozambique
Position	Forward
Club goals	424
International goals	41
Selected honours	Primeira Liga (11 times); Ballon d'Or

THE REFUGEE WHO WON
THE CHAMPIONS LEAGUE

Alphonso Davies was born in a refugee camp in Ghana. His parents, along with half a million others, had fled there to escape a terrible civil war in their home country of Liberia.

A refugee is a person who has to leave their country of origin to avoid terrible danger to themselves. The United Nations made it law that other countries must take in refugees and support them so that they can live in safety and peace – and can contribute as citizens in their new country.

Davies benefited from that law and the kindness of Ghanaians and Canadians when he was accepted as a refugee, relocating to live in Vancouver, Canada.

After excelling for Vancouver Whitecaps, Davies was signed by Bayern Munich and was part of the squad that qualified for the 2020 Champions League final. Munich won, defeating Paris Saint Germain 1–0. At the age of 19, Davies was selected to start, going on to play the whole game.

Davies made his fellow Canadians proud as he was the first from their country to win the Champions League. In addition, he has played 39 times for his country, scoring 13 goals. Contributing wonderfully.

Davies also works as an ambassador for the United Nations High Commission for Refugees.

ALPHONSO DAVIES	
Born	2000, Ghana
Positions	Left-back, winger
Club goals	16
International goals	14
Selected honours	Bundesliga (5 times); Champion's League

ALBERT

In 1965, the same year that Eusébio became the first African to win the Ballon d'Or, the South African player Albert Johanneson became the first person of African heritage to play in the FA Cup final at Wembley, for Leeds United against Liverpool.

Johanneson's 172 games for Leeds United occurred while the club – under manager Don Revie – were emerging as one of the top teams in England and Europe. As a powerful attacking winger, Johanneson scored 48 goals.

Johanneson's appearance in what was then a world-famous football tournament helped begin to change many people's attitudes to Black people in football and society. Although those changes would take decades – and have still not come to fruition entirely.

Racism has remained a problem for decades in football and in society – as we saw with Bukayo Saka in that same Wembley Stadium in 2022.

MANDELA HOSTS
THE WORLD CUP

Football was very important to the prisoners at the Maximum Security Prison on Robben Island, South Africa.

At the time South Africa was run under a system called apartheid, which treated Black people as inferior to white, limiting them opportunity and voice.

A man called Nelson Mandela was in the prison for fighting back against that unfair system. He was held for 26 years and was one of many political prisoners held there.

Mandela said that football made them feel alive when serving a life prison sentence.

In 1994, four years after Mandela's release, he became president, hoping to make South Africa a fairer country. In 2004 he revisited his love of football and helped South Africa win the right to host the 2010 World Cup. This, he knew, could be part of the regeneration of his country.

Many people doubted that an African country could host a sophisticated world sporting event and some tried to challenge the decision.

But they were proved wrong. South Africa 2010 is remembered as a fantastic tournament. No-one who watched it will forget the moment a multi-racial South Africa team ran onto the pitch for the opening match to the sound of vuvuzelas from every corner of the stadium.

THIS IS MY HERO

When Nelson Mandela made an official visit to Leeds in 2001, he was met by the Leeds United and South Africa player, Lucas Radebe. Seeing the captain of his country's football team he announced to those around him, 'This is my hero.'

The following year, Lucas Radebe captained South Africa at the 2002 World Cup finals. A huge honour for any young man. A great moment. But it could so easily have not happened.

Just eleven years before – in 1991 – Radebe's football career and life were almost ended when he was walking with his family in Soweto, his home city. It was a violent city. Radebe has said, 'You heard shots all the time.' It was normal, almost.

Except this time the bullet hit Radebe. He remembered hearing a shot, feeling a pain in his back. Next his left leg stopped working. A bullet had passed through his back and exited through his leg, centimetres from destroying his career and even his life.

To live through that, then to go on to captain your country is an extraordinary thing – and is perhaps is why one of the world's great heroes, Nelson Mandela, called Lucas Radebe his hero.

LUCAS RADEBE	
Born	1969, South Africa
Position	Centre back
Club goals	8
International goals	2
Selected honours	African Cup of Nations

BRINGING THE TROPHY HOME

The FA Cup trophy as we know it was first presented in 1911. A new design – with a broad base and large handles – was created by Bradford jewellers, Fattorini and Sons.

And who were the winners of the trophy that year, lifting the only major trophy they would ever win?

Bradford City.

The coincidence of Bradford City's 1911 FA Cup win is one of many stories that the FA Cup has helped to create since its inception in 1871 during the reign of Queen Victoria, through two world wars, to today's footballing landscape.

Bradford City's 1911 triumph threw up another story, this time a sadder one. The scorer of the only goal in the final was Scottish inside forward, Jimmy Speirs. Four years later – by then a Leeds City player – Speirs volunteered to fight in the First World War. He didn't *have* to fight, as he was married and had two children. But he chose to fight for his country.

Jimmy Speirs was killed at the Battle of Passchendaele in 1917, shot in the thigh.

He will be remembered for his war heroics, but also for winning the FA Cup made in Bradford, for the city of Bradford.

FA CUP FINAL	
Saturday, 22 April 1911	
Bradford City 1–0 Newcastle United	
Jimmy Speirs 15'	

THE KEEPER WITH THE BROKEN NECK

There's a remarkable photograph of the Manchester City goalkeeper, Bert Trautmann, taken just after the end of the 1956 FA Cup final at Wembley, a game City won.

Trautmann is pictured walking across the Wembley football field with two of his teammates. He is holding his neck, but still smiling broadly. He knows he is injured, but not quite how badly.

In fact, his neck is broken in two places.

During the 75th minute, in a collision with a Birmingham City player, Trautmann had been knocked unconscious. He came round and played on to make key saves and help his team win the cup.

With a broken neck.

Trautmann was another footballer whose story spans the beautiful game and the horrors of war. A German soldier in the Second World War, Trautmann was captured by the British and was made a prisoner of war until the end of the conflict.

After the war Trautmann chose to stay in England and was scouted by City. He would end up playing 545 times for them and remains fourth in the list of players who have appeared most times in the Manchester City shirt. Yet he should be placed first when it comes to heroics.

OW!

BERT TRAUTMANN	
Born	1923, Germany
Position	Goalkeeper
Selected honours	FA Cup

DOUBLE SAVE

The 1973 FA Cup final threw up one of the tournament's great shocks, with second-tier Sunderland beating top-flight Leeds United, then holders of the trophy as well as one of the best teams in Europe.

The scorer of the game's only goal was Ian Porterfield. But the real hero, who is remembered to this day on Wearside, was the keeper, Jimmy Montgomery. His double save is considered an equal to Gordon Banks's against Pelé in 1970.

Having parried a powerful goal-bound header by one Leeds player, Montgomery struggled to get to his feet to deal with a volley from Peter Lorimer, who blasted it from inside the six-yard area. Somehow, his body twisted away from the ball, Montgomery pushed the ball up onto the bar, and it was cleared.

Sunderland went on to win 1–0. But shocks are part of why the FA Cup has such a reputation.

IN THE MUD

Earlier in the 1972 FA Cup, top flight Newcastle United travelled to non-league Hereford United having failed to beat them at St James' Park in the first game. It was the third round of the cup, when the big teams join smaller clubs from nine tiers of the English and Welsh game.

Everyone expected Newcastle to put Hereford away in the replay. And it took Newcastle until the 82nd minute to take the lead, thinking they had broken Hereford hearts.

But they had not. Three minutes after Newcastle scored, Ronnie Radford equalised for the team five leagues below Newcastle, forcing extra time. His goal was a long-range blaster that caused hundreds of fans – many children – to join him on the pitch to celebrate. It took the police a while to clear the pitch.

And in extra time it happened.

The substitute – Ricky George – took a pass

with his back to goal, turned in the heavy mud and thumped the ball home, causing more Hereford fans to invade the pitch.

Unbelievable – 2–1. Hereford had killed their giant, although Newcastle would go on to win nothing for the next 50 years. The scenes of fans and players on the pitch have gone down as the ultimate third-round giant killing.

WOO-HOOOOOOOOOOOOO!

FA CUP THIRD ROUND	
Saturday, 5 Feb 1972	
Hereford United 2–1 Newcastle United	
Ronnie Radford 85'	Malcolm Macdonald 82'
Ricky George 103'	

THE CRAZY GANG

When Liverpool walked out at Wembley to play
Wimbledon in the 1988 FA Cup final, they had only
recently been crowned champions of England for the
seventh time in nine years. It remains one of the two
most successful eras of any English club, along with
Manchester United's teams under Sir Alex Ferguson.

Liverpool were fully expected to complete a league
and cup double and become the first English club to
achieve that twice.

Wimbledon – in contrast – had been in the football
league for only 11 years, and in the top flight for only
two. Many of their team had played up through non-
league football as amateurs to reach the pinnacle of
the game.

It was David against Goliath.

Lawrie Sanchez scored a neat header, giving
Wimbledon a 1–0 lead in the first half, but Liverpool
were relentless and were still favourites to win. When

Liverpool won a penalty, it seemed the bubble had burst for Wimbledon. A penalty had never been missed in an FA Cup final before.

John Aldridge stepped up to take the spot kick against the Dons' keeper, Dave Beasant, the first goalkeeper to captain an FA Cup side at Wembley. When Beasant saved the shot – pushing it round his left-hand post – he also became the first keeper to save a penalty in an FA Cup final.

Wimbledon had won the FA Cup. The BBC's legendary commentator John Motson remarked, as the final whistle blew, that 'the Crazy Gang have beaten the Culture Club'.

FA CUP FINAL	
Saturday, 14 May 1988	
Liverpool 0–1 Wimbledon	
	Lawrie Sanchez 37'

LE SPORTSMANSHIP

The FA Cup has a long history of shocks and controversies and things going wrong. But one FA Cup moment stands out as someone doing something right.

When Arsenal scored their winner in a 2–1 defeat of Sheffield United in the fifth round of the 1999 FA Cup, the Yorkshire team were aggrieved. The winning goal had been scored after Sheffield United had kicked the ball out of play so that a player could receive treatment for injury.

The unspoken rule in such a situation is that if a player kicks the ball out so another can receive treatment, the opposing team should return the ball to them.

But that didn't happen. Arsenal's Nwankwo Kanu and Marc Overmars combined to score after the restart. The Sheffield United players and supporters were outraged, but the referee could do nothing. It took eight minutes before the game could restart, such was the disquiet.

After the game finished, Arsenal's French manager, Arsène Wenger, immediately offered to replay the game. His offer was accepted and Arsenal won the next game. Without controversy.

'We feel that it is not right... quite simply, it was not fair,' explained Wenger.

Sportsmanship.

TRÈS BIEN!

FAIR PLAY

In 2019 Leeds United manager Marcelo Bielsa made
a decision that arguably surrendered his team's
automatic promotion, during a late-season game
against Aston Villa.

With the score at 0–0 and with Leeds building
from the back, the Villa forward Jonathan Kodjia
went down injured. Leeds played on as the Villa
players seemed to stop, assuming Leeds would put the
ball out.

Leeds didn't put the ball out and pushed on to
score. The Yorkshire team were now leading 1–0
and still looking good for automatic promotion. This
resulted in booing from the Villa fans, scuffles on
the pitch and an argument between the two sets of
coaching staff.

It was an ugly situation.

Then Leeds' Argentinian manager Bielsa stunned
football by ordering his players to let Villa score from

the restart. Villa kicked off, jogged the ball down the centre of the pitch and knocked it into the net.

It was now 1–1.

And 1–1 was how the game ended. The failure to collect three points meant Leeds would not be promoted that season. Because they had done the right thing.

Leeds were awarded the prestigious FIFA Fair Play Award for 2019.

RESPECT TO SEÑOR BIELSA!

A BORING FACT

This might sound boring, but bear with us.

Before the 1980s a team winning a football match in England would be awarded two points for a win. This meant that teams would often play for a draw and one point, rather than take risks to gain two points, and losing, gaining none.

Some games were boring as a result. Sometimes both teams seemed happy to play for a draw. There were far more 0–0 results.

The former Fulham footballer and TV pundit Jimmy Hill was the first to suggest a change. He believed football would be more exciting if teams were better motivated to try to win and therefore play more attacking football.

The English FA agreed and from 1981 teams would earn three points for a win.

So, yes, it sounds like a boring fact – as boring as two teams playing unadventurous football – but the change sparked English football into life and soon the rest of the world followed. It was used first in the 1994 World Cup and is now standard in football and other sporting league competitions across the world.

Some argue that other changes of rules at around the same time made football more interesting. Such as not allowing keepers to pick up a back pass. And being firmer with players who committed more brutal tackles.

Either way, now football is not as boring.

NO CORNERS, NO KEEPERS, NO CROSSBAR

The first official rules for a game called Association Football were created by the newly formed English Football Association in 1863.

They were drawn up over six meetings in London's Freemasons Tavern, the first meeting taking place on 26 October 1863.

The rules were devised to help make the game different to rugby, which was far more physical and involved handling the ball most of the time, plus a fair amount of long-range kicking.

However, those first rules were not easy to decide on. There were massive disagreements. The biggest row was about hacking. Hacking is when you are allowed to kick at the opposition players' shins as hard as you like. In the end, the teams that wanted to do this were not allowed to join the new game.

Over the years the rules have changed. In 1863 there were no corners, no keepers and no crossbar.

You had to change ends each time a goal was scored. And you were allowed to catch the ball in play and – if you did – you earned a free kick.

But those first rules, created in 1863, became the beginning of what is now recognised as the distinctive sport of association football.

THE WORLD'S FIRST
FOOTBALL CLUB

Recognised by FIFA as the world's first football club, Sheffield FC was formed in 1857 when members of the Sheffield Cricket Club decided to have a kick about.

In doing so they became what is now the world's first football club that still plays today, currently in the Northern Premier League.

Their first games were played amongst themselves. In one game married players competed against single players. In another, professionals – those with fancy jobs – played against 'the rest'.

They joined the Football Association in 1863, but played their own rules until 1868.

Sheffield has been better known for its two league teams, Wednesday (established in 1867) and United (founded 1889), but it is Sheffield FC that will always be able to claim its place in world history.

The world's first football club.

THE FIRST ENGLISH CHAMPIONS

The first women's team to be national English champions was also based in South Yorkshire, just 20 miles from Sheffield, a part of the world that has always been seen as the crucible of football.

Doncaster Belles were founded in 1969 by lottery ticket sellers who worked the games when Doncaster Rovers men's team played their home games at Belle Vue. They quickly became a force in the game and won most leagues and cups they played in for the next 20 years.

Having already won the national cup competition four times, they won the inaugural National Premier Division in its first season of 1991–92 with a 100 per cent record. The Belles also won the FA Cup that year, beating Red Star Southampton 4–0 in the final. To win the league and cup double in the National Premier Division's first year was a great achievement and underlined the Belles' dominance of the game.

The Belles won the league again in 1993–94, and were immortalised in the title of football author Pete Davies's book, *I Lost My Heart to the Belles* (1996). The book helped to overcome the sexist attitudes to women playing football that were widespread in the 1990s and, even now, have still not gone away entirely.

I'VE NOT BEEN GOOD ENOUGH

After a defeat to Germany in England's first qualifying game for the 2002 World Cup, the England manager, Doncaster-born Kevin Keegan, gave an extraordinary interview on live TV.

'I've not been quite good enough,' he said. 'I'm not the man to take it that stage further... and I know that.'

Kevin Keegan was resigning as England manager.

Keegan had been the best English footballer of his generation. He won leagues, cups and the European Cup with Liverpool in their 1970s glory days. He played 63 times for his country, scoring 21 times. He moved to play for Hamburg in the Bundesliga, when British players were famous for not doing well abroad. But Keegan did well. Very well. He won the Ballon d'Or in 1978 and 1979 while playing in Germany.

But in the early 2000s, one game – a defeat – against Germany made him realise that to be England manager you needed something he didn't have. And he said so.

Kevin Keegan knew his limits and he was ready to be honest about that.

KEVIN KEEGAN	
Born	1951, England
Position	Forward
Club goals	204
International goals	21
Selected honours	Football League First Division; FA Cup; European Cup; Bundesliga

ROY OF THE ROVERS STUFF

There is a phrase you'll often hear British football commentators say: *This is Roy of the Rovers stuff.*

They're referring to the world's most famous fictional footballer, Roy Race.

Roy first appeared in a children's comic called *Tiger* in 1954. He was a young striker battling to make a career in the brutal world of the professional game. From 1976 to 1995 he had his own comic, published weekly. He was read by hundreds of thousands of children. And some adults.

The phrase 'Roy of the Rovers stuff' captured the idea of something that was against the odds, impossible, a dream that somehow always came true. Something children could aspire to.

But there was more to Roy than that. He was a role model to those children too. Whatever happened to Roy Race on the pitch, he always tried to do the right thing. He never got booked. He always said sorry if he'd messed up. And he worked hard to do the right thing off the pitch, too.

In the 1960s, he was compared to England World Cup winning captain, Bobby Moore. Today, he could be likened to Marcus Rashford.

In 2018 a new series of graphic novels and fiction featured a modern Roy, 16 again and – equally importantly – with his footballing sister, Rocky Race.

Roy of the Rovers stuff for a new generation.

BE MORE MARCUS

During the Covid pandemic the Manchester United and England footballer, Marcus Rashford, used his fame, his kindness and his intelligence to help families struggling across the UK.

Rashford had a tough upbringing. His mum, a single mother, needed to work several low-paid jobs to feed and clothe her five children, frequently going without food when there was not enough to go round.

Rashford never forgot the deprivations his family suffered. In 2019 he began campaigns and collaborations to help homeless people and children in families where there was not enough money for food. He used his fame to speak out against bad political decisions and to put pressure on the government.

Marcus Rashford was awarded an MBE and many other awards for his work. In a game with many poor role models, Marcus is someone we should all want to be like.

CARDBOARD SUPPORTERS

With the Covid pandemic shutting crowds out of the stadiums, fans were frustrated they could not support their teams. Even when the games were back on, supporters were not yet allowed back in.

So, around the world, football clubs set up schemes where fans could buy a cardboard cut-out of themselves to stand at their seat in the stadium. Thousands of fans did this, motivated not just by being at the game in spirit, but by supporting the charities that this money would go towards.

For instance, 20,000 Borussia Monchengladbach fans paid to have their cut-outs attend home games, raising thousands for charity. Even away fans were invited to offer their support. The money raised would go to charities supported by the Borussia Foundation.

Even in the difficult times of the pandemic, football fans and clubs rose to the occasion.

FOOTBALL'S BACK

Seeing the stadiums full of football supporters again after Covid was a buzz for everyone. Seeing and hearing and feeling the crowds.

England captain Harry Kane talked about how good it was to score a goal and run to celebrate with the fans, and how he had missed that experience on the pitch.

But football is about more than the scorers and the cheering; it's as much about what happens off the pitch. We learned that from Covid – that football was about friends and families going back to do the thing they love the most, following their team, letting it all out for 90 minutes. What was lost through Covid had been found, and it felt all the more important because now we knew what we had been missing.

A Crystal Palace fan called Andy was interviewed after his first game back at Selhurst Park.

'To be able to get back to Selhurst with my

81-year-old dad for the first time meant so much,' he explained. 'We've been going to Palace since the '70s... we go up... we go down... but one thing stays the same... the noise from the stands and my dad next to me.'

That moment of return meant so much to so many people. It reminded them of what football was about.

THE MEXICAN WAVE

Fans are a huge part of the game of football and have helped provide some of the sport's greatest moments. This is never more obvious than when a stadium of those fans delivers a Mexican Wave.

Most of the world was unfamiliar with the stadium wave, as it was known, before the 1986 FIFA men's World Cup in Mexico. Until then, it had been seen mostly in US universities. But when the World Cup was hosted for the second time in Mexico, and fans delivered a wave in match after match, the world embraced the idea and named it the Mexican Wave, whereupon it played out on every continent.

During a wave, each section of the crowd stand and raises arms, then just as rapidly sits down, creating the sense a great wave of people is travelling round the stadium. It forms a sense of togetherness among all the fans which is not always the case in football.

Not everyone joins in the Mexican wave, of course.

Sometimes – with a home team leading by several goals – the wave can stop when it reaches away fans, who might not be in the same celebratory mood.

THE VIKING THUNDER CLAP

A team or country's fans can have a huge impact on how their team performs. In 2016 Iceland qualified for their first major tournament, Euro 2016 in France, beating the Netherlands on the way.

Some argue that it was their fans' extraordinary chant – the Viking Thunder Clap – that helped inspire their qualifying for the Euros and their success in the finals.

The Viking Thunder Clap begins with a loud shout and clap by the fans, then it is repeated faster and faster like a war cry. The effect of hundreds, sometimes thousands of fans doing this, is loud and intimidating. Unless it is your fans that are doing the chant. Then it is invigorating.

Iceland defeated Austria and drew with Portugal and Hungary in the group stages, defying all expectation, then faced England in the Round of 16. With their fans' deep chants resonating around the stadium in Nice, they shocked the English, beating them 2–1. At the time England had a population of 60 million, but Iceland had just 300,000.

The chant's origins have been claimed by clubs in Poland, Greece, France and – most prominently – by Motherwell fans in Scotland. But it will be remembered as the chant that Iceland fans delivered to help their national team defy the odds and reach the quarter-finals of Euro 2016.

CLAP! CLAP! CLAP!

EUROPEAN CHAMPIONSHIPS ROUND OF 16	
Monday, 27 June 2016	
England 1–2 Iceland	
Wayne Rooney 4' (P)	Ragnar Sigurðsson 6'
	Kolbeinn Sigþórsson 18'

THE MATCH OF DEATH?

During the Nazi occupation of Ukraine in the early 1940s there were often football matches. Sometimes those games happened between the occupied and the occupiers.

The story behind one story of these games has stuck. It goes like this.

On 6 August 1942 a Ukrainian team called Start, representing Bread Factory No. 1, beat the German side Flakelf 5–1. The Germans did not like this defeat. It was not good for the 'master race' – as they liked to be perceived – to be seen to be soundly beaten by the servants from the factory who were forced to make their bread.

A rematch was arranged.

Now the Germans insisted the factory workers – some of whom were former Dynamo Kyiv players – had to lose or they would be punished. With death. Intimidated, the Ukrainians trailed 3–1 at half-time.

To live they had to lose.

They story continues that the Ukraine fans in the stadium were outraged their team was losing to a Nazi team. The occupied had to beat the occupiers: to show them and the world that they could not be oppressed. The locals responded to their crowd and scored four times, defeating the Germans 5–3.

In the coming days several of the Start players were executed or sent to forced labour camps. But at least the Ukrainians had shown – again – that they could defeat the Nazis.

Is this story true? Some of it is. But all of it? Probably not. Some historians have tried to get to the bottom of the story of the Match of Death, but the records kept by the Germans were never found and when the Russians took over Ukraine after the war, they may have exaggerated the story too. And those who took part are long gone.

Was Start v Flakelf really a Match of Death? We will never know.

USELESS CREATURES

When Nettie Honeyball set up the British Ladies FC
– with the support of Lady Florence Dixie in 1895 –
she did it because of her love of football, but also as a
political act.

'Women are not the ornamental and useless
creatures that men have pictured,' she said.

Off the pitch women were expected to dress in
a certain way. On the pitch women could be – and
show that they could be – athletes and did not need
to wear corsets and high-heeled boots.

At their first game 11,000 fans turned up to watch
the north beat the south 7–1. An impressive crowd.
A positive start. But there were negatives too that
day. Many of that crowd heckled them, laughing at
women thinking they could play football. And in the
newspapers, they were derided.

Dixie and Honeyball continued to do what they
wanted: using football to challenge attitudes to girls

and women. Seeing far into the future, Lady Dixie predicted that one day it would be as popular for girls to play football as it was for boys.

The British Ladies FC were trailblazers in changes of attitude towards women and equality on and off the football pitch. But the process would take decades and is still not complete.

EQUAL PAY

In 2019, some 124 years after Lady Dixie predicted that girls and boys would be equals on the football field, a group of US women footballers filed a lawsuit against the US Soccer Federation. Having won the Olympic football four times and the World Cup four times they demanded equal pay with US men footballers.

The men had never won either tournament.

Led by high-profile US soccer players Megan Rapinoe and Alex Morgan, the US Women's Soccer Team filed against wage discrimination. They fought in the courts and they campaigned in the media. And at the 2019 World Cup in France their fans joined in, chanting, 'Equal pay! Equal pay!'

Their claim was dismissed by the courts. The answer was no.

But Rapinoe, Morgan and their teammates appealed. They were not going to give up. Elite sports people don't give up.

And in 2022 they won their court case. In the United States men and women would receive equal pay for playing for their national soccer team. As in England, Norway, New Zealand and Australia, footballers representing their countries would receive equal pay regardless of their gender.

FOOTBALL YOUR WAY

The 21st century brought further attempts at removing some of the barriers of inequality for people who wanted to play football – one of which was concerned with how disabled people could access the game.

The English FA was one of several national football bodies that put more thought and action into helping disabled people to enjoy playing the game.

In 2021 they published a plan to develop disability football to allow all fans access to the game on and off the pitch. It was called Football Your Way. And it was a big moment in addressing the needs of disabled people, when it came to football.

Some of their plans included working with blind football, deaf football, cerebral palsy football and powerchair football.

The scheme comes to an end in 2024 and will be revisited then.

FIRST CAP OF 214

Birgit Prinz made her debut for Germany aged 16. She came on as a substitute striker in the-73rd minute, and netted the winner in the 89th minute. It was an astonishing debut that set up an even more astonishing career.

Between 1994 and 2011 Prinz played 214 times for Germany, scoring 128 goals and remains her country's most-capped player and leading goalscorer.

During that time Germany won the European Championship four times and the World Cup twice. Prinz was awarded the FIFA World Player of the Year in 2003, 2004 and 2005 and was runner-up five times.

Prinz had been a catalyst behind a remarkable decade and a half of Germany glory.

But she also achieved off the pitch, qualifying as a physical therapist. She now works as a psychologist in the German Bundesliga.

In the history of the women's World Cup finals, Prinz stands as the second highest scorer in tournaments, with 14 goals, second only to the greatest of all time, Marta.

Quite an achievement for a girl who made her debut for her country aged only 16.

BIRGIT PRINZ	
Born	1977, Germany
Position	Forward
Club goals	282
International goals	128
Selected honours	Bundesliga (9 times); World Cup (2 times); European Championships (5 times)

TALK ABOUT THE GAME, NOT THE REFEREE

In 2021, when Rebecca Welch became the first woman to be selected as referee in the men's English Football League, she said that by the end of the match she wanted people to be talking about the match and not the referee.

The match was between Harrogate Town and Port Vale. And she did acknowledge that her appointment was a huge moment for the game. And for her.

Welch first became a referee in 2010, and had since officiated an FA Cup final and in the Champions League, as well as in international matches.

More recently, she has gone on to referee several EFL games and an FA Cup third round tie between Birmingham City and Plymouth Argyle. She is now one of UEFA's elite referees.

BRONZE WINS GOLD

The women's game in England has been developing fast with the formation of the Women's Super League in 2010. One of the steps on that road to glory was the day in 2020 when England's captain, Lucy Bronze, became the first English player to win Best FIFA Women's Player.

Bronze's achievement came off the back of being one of the English game's great exports. Playing for French super club, Lyon, she was an essential part of their treble winning team of 2020, which won the domestic league and cup double, as well as the Champions League. In addition, she captained an England team that had been improving year on year.

At the same award ceremony, the Netherlands coach, Sarina Wiegman, won coach of the year, just as she prepared to take over as England manager.

With the world's top coach and player in their corner, the future was beginning to look bright for

England. The two women would be instrumental in
taking England to glory at Euro 2022.

LUCY BRONZE	
Born	1991, England
Position	Right-back
Club goals	23
International goals	12
Selected honours	Women's Super League (3 times); Liga F; European Women's Championship

THEY NEVER GAVE UP

On 11 March 2011 Japan suffered a devastating earthquake and tsunami. It was a national catastrophe, in which 20,000 people were killed.

Four months later their women's football team competed in the World Cup final against a USA team packed with star players like Alex Morgan, Megan Rapinoe and Abby Wambach.

The USA were clear favourites, and they would take the lead in the game, after 69 minutes. But Japan equalised after 81. That meant extra time.

In the 104th minute, the USA scored again – but with just three minutes of extra time to go, Japan equalised for a second time. So the final would be decided on penalties!

When Homare Sawa, the Japan captain, received the trophy after a 3–1 penalty shoot-out win, she took it to her teammates and they lifted it as one. As a team. As a country.

After the game, Abby Wambach, the USA striker, explained why they lost to their opponents. 'They never gave up,' she said.

Japan had become the first team from Asia ever to lift a World Cup in football, men or women.

A huge moment for world football.

WORLD CUP FINAL	
Sunday, 17 July 2011	
Japan 2–2 USA	
Aya Miyama 81'	Alex Morgan 69'
Homare Sawa 117'	Abby Wambach 104'
Japan won 3–1 on penalties	

SOUTH KOREA AND JAPAN HOST MEN'S WORLD CUP

The first 16 men's World Cup finals competitions were hosted either by a country in Europe (nine times) or in the Americas (seven times). Some might have objected to calling it the World Cup.

At first it looked like the 17th World Cup in 2002 might be staged in Mexico for a third time, as they were competing with separate bids from South Korea and Japan, and appeared to be favourites. But then someone had the idea to combine South Korea and Japan's bids. The two countries are relatively close to each other on the edge of south-east Asia and it made such good sense that they received unanimous support.

And so the first men's World Cup to be played in Asia was scheduled. This was a big moment in football. To break away from the traditional host countries was a way to make football more global, to inspire more countries to play the game and watch the game.

Since Asia hosted the men's World Cup in 2002, the tournament has taken place in Africa, Asia again and in the Middle East. At last it's a global tournament.

For the record, incidentally, the first ever FIFA women's World Cup was hosted in 1991 by China.

GIVE THAT MAN
A KNIGHTHOOD

We've played two and a half minutes of stoppage time. The commentator's voice is tense. *England trail by two goals to one. Beckham could raise the roof here with a goal...*

England's men's team are losing 2–1 to Greece at Old Trafford. They need a draw to qualify for the 2002 World Cup finals in South Korea and Japan. This is the so-called Golden Generation including players like Steven Gerrard, Rio Ferdinand and David Beckham.

With time running out, Teddy Sheringham wins a free kick 30 yards out and wants to take it. The regular free kick taker, Beckham, has already failed to score from six free kicks in the game – but he gathers the ball and places it. Focusing. Believing.

Sixty-six thousand spectators hold their breath in the stadium, along with millions of England fans at home and in pubs up and down the country, as David

Beckham turns the ball over in his hands, places it, then takes a few steps back.

He puts his hands on his hips. He waits. The referee blows his whistle. One, two, three steps. Beckham strikes the ball. It sails over the Greek wall. There's a half-second of silence from the crowd. Then a deafening roar.

I don't believe it, the commentator screams. David Beckham scores the goal to take England all the way to the World Cup finals. Give that man a knighthood.

David Beckham has scored one of the great British goals in history.

DAVID BECKHAM	
Born	1975, England
Position	Midfielder
Club goals	97
International goals	17
Selected honours	Premier League (5 times); La Liga; Ligue 1; Champions League

BICYCLE KICK

The greatest goal ever scored in a Champions League final was arguably Gareth Bale's first for Real Madrid in the 2018 final against Liverpool.

The score was 1–1 with both goals being scored early in the second half. The match had come to life. Then after 63 minutes a ball was played out wide to Real's left back, Marcelo Vieira. The Brazilian international controlled the pass and fired it across the penalty area... to where the Welsh international, Gareth Bale was waiting close to the penalty spot. A good 12 yards out.

Would Bale control it, try to turn and shoot? Would he head it down to a teammate to have a strike? Neither. Surprising everyone, the Welshman leaped into the air, his back to the goal, and performed the most remarkable overhead – or bicycle – kick, catching the ball with his left foot and volleying it into the top left corner of the goal.

Watching footage of it you can see the Real Madrid fans. At first, they don't celebrate. Did they doubt such a strike was possible? The fans who had enjoyed such players as Luka Modrić, Cristiano Ronaldo and Karim Benzema over the last decade had to look twice before they celebrated.

Now Real led 2–1. Twenty minutes later Bale scored again. Liverpool were defeated – and Real Madrid were European champions for the 13th time.

GARETH BALE	
Born	1989, Wales
Position	Forward
Club goals	141
International goals	41
Selected honours	La Liga (3 times); Champions League (5 times)

BARNES IN BRAZIL

Throughout the history of football Brazil had been celebrated for entertaining, attacking football. Meanwhile, England had been recognised as providing more functional football, meaning that they got the job done without too much flair.

Those notions were turned on their head one day in 1984 when John Barnes, the England international, made his first appearance at Brazil's famous Maracanã stadium in Rio. It was his tenth performance for England.

Brazil, away. The toughest game you could hope to play in.

To make matters worse, England had an abysmal record against Brazil. Out of the last eleven times the two teams had met, Brazil had won seven and the rest had been draws. At the time, England had only ever beaten Brazil once. In 1956.

Then Barnes arrived.

He received the ball just inside Brazil's half of the pitch. He took it gently with his head so that it fell to his feet, just ahead of him. And then he attacked, accelerating through the Brazil midfield, then angling into the penalty area, outpacing three defenders, rounding the keeper and touching it into the net.

It was a truly great goal. Unexpected. An unfancied team doing something extraordinary and outrageous.

INTERNATIONAL FRIENDLY	
Sunday, 10 June 1984	
Brazil	England
	John Barnes 44'
	Mark Hateley 65'

GOAL OF THE SEASON

Justin Fashanu's beautiful strike against Liverpool in 1980 was made English football's Goal of the Season and he is remembered fondly by fans of the game who were around to see it on *Match of the Day*.

Fashanu was also remarkable for another reason. In an era of homophobia, where gay people were routinely horribly mocked and abused from the terraces, he was the first footballer to come out as gay.

Even today very few male footballers have come out as gay and it is testament to Fashanu's bravery that he did so more than 40 years ago.

The goal. His defining moment on the pitch.

Fashanu had his back to goal with legendary Liverpool defender, Alan Kennedy, behind him. The Norwich City player flicked the ball up with his right foot, and as it dropped, he turned and volleyed the ball over the keeper and into the top left-hand corner of the net. The keeper was Ray Clemence of Liverpool and England, the best of his generation.

It is the kind of goal that words can never do justice to.

Justin Fashanu, who died in 1997, was inducted into the National Football Museum's Hall of Fame in 2020.

FASHANUUUUUUUUUUUU!

JUSTIN FASHANIU	
Born	1961, England
Position	Forward
Club goals	133

MORE TALES OF
THE UNEXPECTED

In some sports, the big teams and big players always win, and the little ones don't. But one of the great things about football is the unexpected. Something could happen that no-one saw coming.

When the Premier League's 2015–16 season began, the previous 20 competitions had been won by only four teams: Arsenal, Chelsea, Manchester City and Manchester United. Teams with a history of winning, and millions of supporters worldwide to bankroll that success. The Premier League was becoming as predictable as the top flight in Spain and Scotland.

But not in 2015–16. In that season, the Premier League was won by... Leicester City. The closest they had previously come to that achievement was second place in 1928–29.

Leicester's odds at the beginning of the season were 5,000–1. They were a team with no superstars and an initially unpopular manager, Claudio Ranieri, but

they won 23 of their games, drew 12, and lost three –
once to Liverpool and twice to Arsenal.

These tales of the unexpected come every so often
into football, making it the great game it is.

PREMIER LEAGUE 2015/16								
TEAM	PI	W	D	L	F	A	GD	Pts
Leicester City	38	23	12	3	68	36	32	81
Arsenal	38	20	11	7	65	36	29	71
Tottenham Hotspur	38	19	13	6	69	35	34	70
Manchester City	38	19	9	10	71	41	30	66

THE DOUBLE

Although it has been achieved many times in recent years the first team to win the men's English double since 1900 – winning the league and the FA Cup in one season – was Tottenham Hotspur.

In the early days of the game – when there were fewer teams in the competition – the double had been won by Preston and Aston Villa. But the feat had not been achieved in the 92-team modern game for over 60 years.

Until Spurs in 1961.

At that time, and with so many clubs capable of winning trophies, the double was considered to be an almost impossible achievement.

But Spurs did it in style, winning 31 games from 42, scoring 115 goals, conceding 55. Their manager Bill Nicholson and captain Danny Blanchflower became legends of the game.

Since the apparently impossible was achieved by

Spurs, more and more teams have won the double. Chelsea and Liverpool have won it once, Manchester City twice and Man U and Arsenal three times.

FOOTBALL LEAGUE FIRST DIVISION 1960/61								
TEAM	Pl	W	D	L	F	A	GD	Pts
Tottenham Hotspur	42	31	4	7	115	55	60	66
Sheffield Wednesday	42	23	12	7	78	47	31	58
Wolverhampton Wanderers	42	25	7	10	103	75	28	57
Burnley	42	22	7	13	102	77	25	51

THE DOUBLE DOUBLE

When Manchester United won the double in 1993–
94 – setting up two decades of dominance in the
English game – their manager Alex Ferguson achieved
something even more remarkable.

Ferguson was a double double winner.

Ferguson's success at Manchester United was
extraordinary as they won 24 major trophies during
his years in charge. But his success as manager of
Aberdeen in Scotland could be thought of as even
more remarkable.

In Scotland, the two Glasgow teams – Rangers and
Celtic – had dominated both the league and the cup
and still do. For another team to win the league was a
rare occasion. For another team to win the league and
the cup was unheard of.

But in 1983 Alex Ferguson had already achieved
that with Aberdeen, taking his unfashionable team on
to win a European trophy too, the Cup Winners' Cup,

adding to his three league titles and four FA cup wins.

The history books and fans remember teams and players more than they do managers. But that is not the case with Sir Alex Ferguson, either in Scotland or in England.

And that double double moment – when Ferguson won it a second time with Manchester United – stands out as something that has never been matched in British football.

SIR ALEX FERGUSON	
Born	1941, Scotland
Position	Forward
Club goals	171
International goals	3
Selected honours (as manager)	Premier League (13 times); Champions League (3 times)

CLOUGH AND TAYLOR

Another manager who took a team to unexpected heights was Brian Clough. When the plain-speaking Clough arrived at Nottingham Forest as their new manager in 1975, they were in what was then the second division, now known as the Championship.

During Clough's second full season as manager – 1976–77 – Forest were promoted. Then they did what no team has done since. In the 1977–78 season they became English champions in their first season back in the top league.

But their progress did not end there.

As English champions they qualified for the 1978–79 European Cup. Only champions and the winners of the European Cup could qualify in the days before the tournament morphed into the Champions' League.

Forest won that too, defeating champions Liverpool in the first round.

As winners in 1978–79, they qualified to compete in the 1979–80 European Cup. And won it again.

But those glory years were not achieved alone. Although Clough's finest moments made him the managerial legend he remains today, with statues of him in both Derby and Nottingham, they were achieved in partnership with his assistant, Peter Taylor.

It is hard to believe that a team could be promoted from the second tier, win the top tier the next year, then the European Cup the year after that, and then the same again.

But they did.

INTERNATIONAL
RECORD BREAKER

In March 2023, the Portuguese footballer, Cristiano Ronaldo, made history, breaking two records in one game. The game was a UEFA Euro 2024 qualifier against Liechtenstein.

The first record Ronaldo broke was that he had overtaken the Kuwait international player Bader Al-Mutawa's record for the most appearances as a full international man for his country. Mutawa was on 196 for Kuwait, but Ronaldo had now played 197 times for Portugal. To play that many times for your country shows that you have – over many years – been one of the best that country has to offer. And there is no doubt that Ronaldo was that.

But if you needed any more evidence that Ronaldo is not only one of the greatest Portuguese players in history, but in the world, you should check out the other record he broke that day.

In scoring twice Ronaldo broke his own record of

most goals scored by an international footballer in his career. He moved up from 120 to 122.

Not quite the 214 appearances and 128 goals Birgit Prinz achieved for women's football in Germany, but Ronaldo, as it stands, holds both records for most caps and most goals among men who have played for their countries.

CRISTIANO RONALDO	
Born	1985, Portugal
Position	Forward
Club goals	726
International goals	141
Selected honours	Premier League (3 times); La Liga (2 times); Seria A (2 times); Champions League (5 times)

ZLATAN, THE NUMBERS

There are a lot of numbers attached to the footballing life of the Swedish international, Zlatan Ibrahimović. He's had a long career.

He has played for ten teams, including for his country. The highlights of his list of club teams reads like a list of Europe's greatest: Ajax, Juventus, Inter Milan, Barcelona, AC Milan, Juventus, PSG and Manchester United.

He has been nominated for the Ballon d'Or 11 times. But has never won it. Mainly because he shared the stage with Messi and Ronaldo for his entire career.

He has won the league championship in four different countries: the Netherlands, Italy, Spain and France.

He has played 122 times for Sweden and has scored 62 goals.

When he released an album it reached number 13 in the Swedish charts. It was called *Du gamla, du fria.*

Which translates from Swedish as *You are old, you are free*.

Which leads us to another significant number in Ibrahimović's career. In March 2023 he was selected for the Sweden national squad at the age of 41.

ZLATAN IBRAHIMOVIĆ	
Born	1981, Sweden
Position	Forward
Club goals	405
International goals	62
Selected honours	Eredivisie (2 times); Serie A (5 times); La Liga; Ligue 1 (4 times)

COSMOS

If you were to make up a team of the greatest ever footballers, you might end up with a side including the likes of Pelé, Maradona, Cruyff, Beckenbauer, Yashin, Messi and Ronaldo.

To have just two of those players in one side would be a great moment for the fans lucky enough to be in the stadium.

But it happened in 1977 when Pelé and Beckenbauer turned out for the New York Cosmos in the North American Soccer League, a new venture in the USA to make men's football as popular as some of the other games they like to play in the States: basketball, baseball, American football.

Around the same time a pair of players almost as remarkable played for the Los Angeles Aztecs: Johan Cruyff and George Best.

CAPTAIN MBAPPÉ

When two players considered by many to be the greatest of all time reach the end of their careers, fans and pundits like to look for the next GOAT.

With Ronaldo in his twilight years and Messi leaving PSG in 2023, one current candidate has, at the age of 24, lifted the World Cup and scored in two World Cup finals.

Kylian Mbappé had already played 66 times for his country, scoring 36 goals and had played more than 150 times for PSG, scoring two goals every three games.

Superb stats.

Perhaps because of those stats, or because of his composure and maturity for one still quite young, in March 2023 the France men's manager appointed Mbappé as captain for the Euro 2024 qualifying campaign. In his first game as leader, Mbappé scored twice, and assisted with another goal as France beat the Netherlands 4–0.

If how a player begins the next stage of his career is an indicator of whether he will become one of the game's greatest, then Mbappé is perhaps destined to become the next GOAT.

KYLIAN MBAPPÉ	
Born	1988, France
Position	Forward
Club goals	138
International goals	40
Selected honours	Ligue 1 (6 times); World Cup

HAALAND IN DREAMLAND

When Erling Haaland signed for Manchester City ahead of the 2022–23 season he was wanted by all the big teams in world football. Real Madrid came close to signing him. But Haaland – who was born in Leeds – wanted to return to England to follow his dreams.

And that dream was to join the manager considered by many to be the greatest living football coach: Pep Guardiola at Manchester City.

Although City had dominated English football for a few years, winning seven Premier League titles in eleven years, they had won just one FA Cup in that time and had no success in Europe.

Haaland was signed to help make Manchester City's European dreams come true. To create that great moment.

During the 2022–23 season, Haaland scored 52 goals in 52 appearances, breaking the record for most goals in a Premier League season with 36 goals in 35 appearances. He won both Footballer of the Year and Young Footballer of the Year. He was just 22years old when he achieved this.

Manchester City won a treble of the Premier League, the FA Cup and the Champions League that season, all their dreams coming true after the signing of the Norwegian.

But have all Erling Haaland's dreams come true?

It seems not. In 2017 he gave an interview to a Norwegian newspaper, in which he declared: 'The dream is to win the Premier League with Leeds.'